BLUE HORIZONS

Paradise Isles of the Pacific

Prepared by the Special Publications Division
National Geographic Society, Washington, D. C.

BLUE HORIZONS: PARADISE ISLES OF THE PACIFIC

Contributing Authors: RON FISHER, CHRISTINE ECKSTROM LEE, GENE S. STUART

Contributing Photographers: PAUL CHESLEY, NICHOLAS DEVORE III, DAVID HISER

Published by The National Geographic Society
GILBERT M. GROSVENOR, *President*
MELVIN M. PAYNE, *Chairman of the Board*
OWEN R. ANDERSON, *Executive Vice President*
ROBERT L. BREEDEN, *Vice President, Publications and Educational Media*

Prepared by The Special Publications Division
DONALD J. CRUMP, *Editor*
PHILIP B. SILCOTT, *Associate Editor*
WILLIAM L. ALLEN, *Senior Editor*

Staff for this book
MARGERY G. DUNN, *Managing Editor*
THOMAS B. POWELL III, *Picture Editor*
LYNETTE R. RUSCHAK, *Art Director*
PATRICIA F. FRAKES, CAROLINDA E. HILL, *Researchers*
RON FISHER, CHRISTINE ECKSTROM LEE, THOMAS O'NEILL, GENE S. STUART, *Picture Legend Writers*
SALLY J. BENSUSEN, *Flower Art*
SUSAN SANFORD, *Map Art*

JOHN D. GARST, JR., JOSEPH F. OCHLAK, JAMES V. MAUCK, KEVIN Q. STUEBE, *Map Research and Production*
PAMELA B. TOWNSEND, *Editorial Assistant*
ARTEMIS S. LAMPATHAKIS, *Illustrations Assistant*

Engraving, Printing, and Product Manufacture
ROBERT W. MESSER, *Manager*
GEORGE V. WHITE, *Production Manager*
GEORGE J. ZELLER, JR., *Production Project Manager*
MARK R. DUNLEVY, DAVID V. SHOWERS, GREGORY STORER, *Assistant Production Managers;* MARY A. BENNETT, *Production Assistant*

ELIZABETH ANN BRAZEROL, DIANNE T. CRAVEN, CAROL ROCHELEAU CURTIS, LORI E. DAVIE, MARY ELIZABETH DAVIS, ANN DI FIORE, EVA A. DILLON, ROSAMUND GARNER, BERNADETTE L. GRIGONIS, ANNE HAMPFORD, VIRGINIA W. HANNASCH, NANCY J. HARVEY, JOAN HURST, KATHERINE R. LEITCH, CLEO E. PETROFF, VIRGINIA A. WILLIAMS, ERIC W. WILSON, *Staff Assistants*
JEFFREY A. BROWN, *Indexer*

Page 1: Adorned with hibiscus blossoms and a boar's tusk necklace, a Fiji islander beams a broad smile that tells visitors "Bula!—Welcome!"
DAVID HISER

Pages 2-3: Forested volcanic peaks tower above a palm-trimmed shore on Tahiti, a paradise setting epitomizing the natural splendor of French Polynesia.
NICHOLAS DEVORE III

Pages 6-7: Pacific sunset silhouettes Bora Bora, encircled by a tranquil lagoon. Author James Michener called this "the most beautiful island in the world."
NICHOLAS DEVORE III

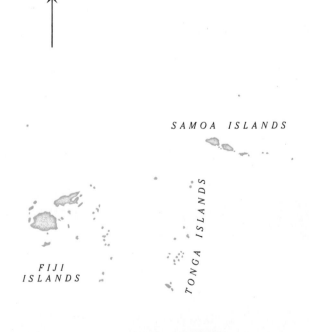

N

SAMOA ISLANDS

TONGA ISLANDS

FIJI ISLANDS

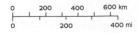

| 0 | 200 | 400 | 600 km |
| 0 | | 200 | 400 mi |

HAWAIIAN ISLANDS

NORTH PACIFIC OCEAN

EQUATOR

SOUTH PACIFIC OCEAN

MARQUESAS
ISLANDS

COOK ISLANDS

TUAMOTU ARCHIPELAGO

SOCIETY ISLANDS

AUSTRAL ISLANDS

GAMBIER
ISLANDS

Contents

Foreword

I was born and grew up in Samoa, referred to in this book as "the spiritual and cultural heart of Polynesia." I have traveled throughout Polynesia, and have lived in many parts of it. I am rooted firmly in it; it nourishes my spirit, helps to define me, and feeds my imagination. For me, Polynesia is not a remote and exotic place: It is home, with all the joys, problems, laughter, pain, and hopes that go with a home.

Our region is a huge scatter of atolls and volcanic islands stretching from Rapa Nui (Easter Island) in the east to Aotearoa (New Zealand) in the south, and north to Hawaii. In Fiji, Polynesia merges with Melanesia. Though most of our cultures flowed from the same fountainhead, our region has brought forth, over the centuries, a rich variety of ways of seeing and interpreting the human condition in relation to nature and the cosmos. Ours is also an assortment of social, economic, and political systems, most of them undergoing different stages of decolonization. We prefer not to be called Pacific islanders or Polynesians: We are Samoans, Tongans, Fijians, Maoris. Most of us do not even understand one another's languages. What binds us together is our generous and benevolent mother, Moana Roa—the Pacific Ocean—and the ancient plaited rope of history that takes us back to a common ancestry, common gods.

No one, not even the gods, can ever know our region in all her manifestations, because whenever we think we have captured her she has already assumed new guises; the love affair is endless because she is always changing. In the final instance, all peoples, cultures, nations, and regions are what we *imagine* them to be at any chosen time. How *papalagi,* the outsiders, perceive and imagine us to be is not necessarily how we, the insiders, see ourselves.

Throughout history, people everywhere have had their own versions of "paradise" and, in their own ways, have searched for that mythical center, that haven over the horizon where their hearts would find meaning and a measure of peace and contentment. That search was probably one of the reasons why our ancestors left home—somewhere in Southeast Asia—and, over centuries of courageous voyaging and discovery and settlement, peopled Polynesia and parts of Melanesia.

For a long time now, papalagi have come to our islands in search of paradise, that place which, they believe, does not suffer from the ills of home. Many left to pursue the dream elsewhere; some stayed and became a strand in the rope of our history; many continue to come. This expatriate quest, motivated by what one writer has called "a dream of islands," has produced a large body of literature which, no matter how fanciful and escapist some of it is, has allowed—and still allows—thousands of stay-at-homes to live out their dream of islands vicariously.

Blue Horizons is in the National Geographic tradition of taking readers to distant places. It looks at six island groups: the Samoas, Tonga, Fiji, French Polynesia, the Cook Islands, and Hawaii. It continues the story of the papalagi's quest for a tropical paradise and, with sensitivity and insight, reveals more about the papalagi's fascination and love affair with our islands. For people not of Polynesia this book is a sympathetic introduction to the islands as they are today. We of the Pacific can read it and, once again, learn more about how papalagi see us—and themselves.

Albert Wendt

Professor of Pacific Literature, The University of the South Pacific, Suva, Fiji

Solitary fisherman awaits a strike on Ofu Island in American Samoa. People of Polynesia treasure the emerald peaks, blue lagoons, and palm-fringed shores of their beloved homelands; visitors find fulfillment of island dreams.

DAVID HISER

9

THE SAMOA ISLANDS

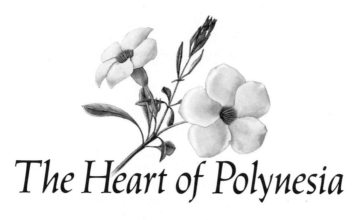

The Heart of Polynesia

By Gene S. Stuart
Photographs by David Hiser

The first miracle of creation was fragrance, according to ancient myth. Then Le Tagaloa, the supreme god, rolled gigantic stones from heaven into the tropic sea. They became islands. Flying clouds married clear heavens and among their progeny were shadow, daylight, and sunset. People developed from creatures of the sea and land. Chiefs descended from gods. And they called their sweet-smelling land Samoa—Sacred Center.

To this day, the Samoa Islands remain the spiritual and cultural heart of Polynesia, though not its geographical center. They lie near the western edge of that vast triangular area stretching from New Zealand northward to Hawaii and eastward to Easter Island.

For some 2,700 years Samoans lived apart from the outside world. But beginning in the 18th century Europeans in sailing ships miraculously appeared along their shores. Dutch explorer Jacob Roggeveen probably came first, in 1722, to prowl the waters and then disappear. Samoans reasoned that these visitors had broken through the sky or had somehow lifted its edge and slipped beneath it. They called the strangers *papalagi*—sky-bursters.

According to one account, frightened natives offered food to appease the gods who had sent the ships from spirit-land. One courageous group boarded a vessel lying offshore and later gave their views of the Europeans—their clothing, footwear, and food: "They found a new race of men, white in colour, dwelling in 'caves' beneath the ship, their skin covered with 'bags,' and 'no toes on their feet.' And from the fact that pieces of pork, supposed to be human flesh, were seen hanging up on the vessel, the new-comers were described as man-eaters."

European impressions of the golden-skinned Samoans were hardly

Gossamer cascade, Fuipisia Falls plunges 185 feet through luxuriant rain forest on Upolu Island in Western Samoa; waders venture near the precipice.
PRECEDING PAGES: *Palms shade Tafua, a village in Western Samoa. Thatched houses called* fale *stay open to ocean breezes; lowered mats bar sun or rain. One family may have three fale: guesthouse, living quarters, and kitchen.*
FLOWER ART: GOLDEN TRUMPET (*Allamanda cathartica*)

13

reassuring. The French explorer Jean François de Galaup, Comte de La Pérouse, and some of his sailors landed on the island of Tutuila in 1787. They were the first foreigners to go ashore in Samoa. Historian K. R. Howe writes that La Pérouse ". . . was staggered at what he considered the 'colossal proportions' of the Samoans, who, for their part, mocked the Frenchmen's smallness. . . ." Warriors killed 12 of the landing party. La Pérouse escaped to tell of the islands' awesome beauty and savage people.

Soon after the arrival of the Reverend John Williams of the London Missionary Society in 1830, Le Tagaloa became Jehovah, and foreign attitudes changed drastically. Nineteenth-century romantics fantasized about enchanted islands and noble savages. Samoa was paradise on earth. Visitors came, lured by visions of a sun-filled Eden—rich volcanic isles where food was for the plucking, where rainbow coral reefs ringed blue lagoons and tropic blossoms perfumed the balmy air. One traveler, Robert Louis Stevenson, found in Samoa the island fantasies of his boyhood.

*I*n his later years, Stevenson lived high on a volcanic mountain slope of Upolu Island, above the port town of Apia and its broad harbor. In 1891 he wrote to a friend, "The place is beautiful beyond dreams; some fifty miles of the Pacific spread in front; deep woods all round; a mountain making in the sky a profile of huge trees upon our left; about us, the little island of our clearing. . . . and the moon . . . makes the night a piece of heaven."

I first saw that clearing in sunlight. Massive teak trees dapple the drive leading to the wide lawns that surround Stevenson's house. A rambling two-story structure, it has been the residence of Western Samoa's head of state since 1962. Mount Vaea—in myth, a lovelorn giant transformed into earth—soars to 1,148 feet above it. When Stevenson died in 1894, grieving Samoans placed him in a tomb on Vaea's summit.

Stevenson often traveled to Apia, now the capital of independent Western Samoa, a nation encompassing the two large islands of Upolu and Savai'i and seven smaller ones. Most towns and villages lie along the coast. I journeyed into Upolu's lush interior, climbing high above Stevenson's home, past plantations of coconut, banana, and taro into forests of planted mahogany. Streams cascade through dark ravines, and white waterfalls plunge from volcanic heights. Clouds enfold the cool rain forest of the mountainous central ridge, where lofty banyan trees wear bromeliads and orchids in their branches like festive garlands.

Stevenson embraced more than an idyllic setting. He adopted, said a turn-of-the-century writer, "a land of poetry—a land where it is 'always afternoon'—and for its size and population there are perhaps more poets here than in any other part of the world." He settled in a land that loves orators and storytellers, proverbs and metaphors, jokes and puns. He learned the musical languages, both the everyday vernacular and the formal chiefly dialect. Knowing the people's love of the supernatural, he translated his short story "The Bottle Imp" into Samoan. It was the first fiction printed in the native tongue. He met with chiefs, made speeches in Samoan, and, perhaps most important, saw the "noble savages" as human beings. They took him into their hearts. They called him *Tusitala*—Teller of Tales.

Western Samoan author Albert Wendt spoke to me of his people's love of words. "Storytelling is Polynesia's most developed art form," he said.

"And ours is the most highly developed verbal art form in the region. Oral literature has always been very important.

"I grew up with a remarkable old woman, my grandmother, who lived with us until she was 94. Every evening she would tell a story to my brothers and me—legends and myths, family history, our genealogies, stories of the forest and the sea. She was a strong Christian, but to her the universe was a mixture of old ghosts, modern ghosts, spirits. And stories were a way of life bonding her to a universe that was real. For me, it was not only what she said, but also who she was and who she represented. She handed me a concept—a whole feeling for what life's all about, especially in the Samoan way, which we call *fa'a Samoa.* My generation was probably one of the last to grow up with people conversant with tradition who told stories."

I was fortunate to encounter fa'a Samoa—the Samoan way—through a young talking chief, an orator, Tusi Va'a Lua. Tusi is the brother of chiefs. He is the great-grandson, grandson, and son of chiefs, all titled Va'a. In Apia he invited me to visit his family in the village of Sale'aula on Savai'i, Western Samoa's largest and most traditional island. It lies 13 miles and 15 minutes by air off Upolu's west coast. Rising between the two, the green, conical islands of Manono and Apolima seemed gleaming stepping-stones in a sunlit garden of reefs. Above the grassy landing strip, Savai'i hid its mountainous interior in a mysterious cover of cloud.

The highlands remain largely untouched, but a modern road encircles the island to link ancient villages. We boarded a bus with wooden benches for a bone-shattering ride northward along the edge of the jagged coast.

There are no walls in a traditional Samoan house, or *fale.* Posts rise from an oval base of volcanic stone to support a roof of thatch or tin. The fale is open to breezes, sunlight, dogs, chickens, the glances of neighbors, and the stares of travelers. As we rattled by, I could see residents napping, weaving pandanus-leaf mats, or sitting and talking. Many waved and smiled. Only hot sun and foul weather are shut out of a fale—by lowering mats that hang beneath the eaves.

Some dwellings are wooden-walled bungalows known as hurricane houses, since they often replace fale destroyed by violent storms. Whatever the house type, each sandy yard is immaculately swept, each green lawn evenly clipped. Beds of flowers and shrubs with leaves as bright as blossoms lie beneath colorful hibiscus bushes and perfumed frangipani trees. Enormous churches, most of them Protestant, dominate each settlement. Slender coconut palms stretch their fringe of leaves toward the sea.

We passed through dark, uninhabited rain forest and then over a rocky

Western Samoa, with a population of some 162,000, gained independence from New Zealand in 1962. The 35,000 residents of American Samoa, a territory since 1900, live in the most southerly of U. S.-held lands.

Savai'i

Apia

Upolu

WESTERN SAMOA

0   20   40   60 km

0   20   40 mi

AMERICAN SAMOA

Tutuila

Pago Pago

Olosega

Ofu

Tau

MANUA ISLANDS

bed where a river no longer flows. A stream of once molten rock parallels the dry riverbed. We crossed the miles-wide moonscape of black lava that disappears into the turquoise sea. The village of Sale'aula lies at its western edge on the shore of a wide lagoon.

Tusi's extended family has three fale, one behind the other, each progressively smaller and less formal—a combined guesthouse and meetinghouse, a dining and family sleeping house, and a kitchen.

"Papalagi, palagi—foreigner," whispered wide-eyed children as I arrived. During my visit one youngster never stopped shrieking and running to the shelter of her grandmother's skirts whenever our eyes met.

Speeches marked my arrival. As my orator, Tusi introduced me; as spokesman for Va'a, the chief, the oldest brother made me welcome—all according to age-old tradition. Va'a presided, the ideal chief, or *matai*. Each extended family chooses its own matai. He must be dignified, patient, and understanding. He must be the steward of communal land, provide food and clothing when needed, and lead impartially in every phase of life. If he fails, the family rescinds the honor and names another.

As much as is possible for a guest, I entered the daily routine, helping care for babies while women cleaned fale and did laundry. Tusi traded his pinstripe trousers of Apia for a brightly flowered *lavalava,* a wraparound garment, and accompanied Va'a to a family plantation of coconut and fruit trees and root crops. In the afternoon I donned a lavalava to swim in the lagoon. I watched from shore as Tusi raced through shallow water with a stick, driving fish into the nets his brothers held. For our evening meal, men arranged breadfruit, taro, and fish on a layer of hot rocks in a ground oven and covered them with broad leaves.

At sunset, the mournful sound of a conch-shell trumpet, once the mystic voice of Samoan war gods, signaled the village *sa,* or prayer time. Families gathered in fale for evening devotions. Speeches of supplication, prayers of gratitude, and the soaring harmonies of hymns came from our family circle, then were repeated from other fale as blue darkness fell.

Only one custom proved frustrating—bath time. Armed with soap and towel, I confronted the water faucet near the small kitchen fale. Samoans bathe and change clothes gracefully and modestly beneath a towel. My efforts resembled the movements of a kitten playing in a paper bag. The family watched in silence, appalled. Literally in a lather and still fully dressed, I upended a basin of water over myself. "You sure you finished?" Tusi asked anxiously. I stalked dripping to the large fale to change clothes beneath a bed sheet.

After evening meals, Tusi and I sat apart in the large fale. I recorded the day's happenings. As a talking chief elected only three months before, Tusi composed speeches in the formal chiefly language, and Va'a joined us to listen, correct, compliment, and advise as Tusi read them aloud. The orations had the sound of songs—poetic testament to the state of being Samoan. Tusi records folk tales as he knows them: stories of lovers and heroes and human frailties in the time of living gods. He memorizes traditional history and genealogy going back to the time when Lealali, a matai descended from the god Le Tagaloa, and his sons came as the first chiefs to inhabit Savai'i.

At night, the family and I stretched out on layers of soft mats and wound ourselves in sheets. I thought of an ancient Samoan belief: Sleep comes when the soul leaves the body to seek clouds and blend with them, for they are its parents and made of the same vapor. Soft winds stirred the palm leaves. The surf whispered from the distant reef. At dawn we woke to brush away the salt powder night breezes had left on our faces.

One morning I walked with Tusi across the silent wasteland at the edge of Sale'aula, across the stony lava flows that have the sheen of satin, the sharpness of obsidian. The village used to spread farther eastward, but in 1905 rivers of molten lava from Mount Matavanu, a volcano eight miles away in the highlands, began flowing to the sea. The eruptions continued until 1911. Lava covered five miles of shoreline. By then, most families, Va'a's among them, had fled and resettled on Upolu.

Talking chief Tusi Va'a Lua cradles his year-old son Loto'olo; his father, high chief Va'a Lua, rests on mats in the family fale in Sale'aula, Western Samoa. Each extended family chooses such leaders, who distribute land, advise members, and make village decisions in council with peers.

FOLLOWING PAGES: *Smoke from early morning cooking drifts beyond villagers walking a narrow dirt road in Upolu's sparsely populated highlands.*

17

"This was part of our family land," Tusi said with a sweep of his hand from sea to forest. We explored the ruins of a London Missionary Society building, newly completed by Vaʻa's grandfather when disaster struck. The surge of lava had broken down the doors and filled the structure to within inches of the windowsills.

Just beyond the edge of the lava, we paused near a sandy mound where grave lay upon grave. "My family still uses our old burial ground," Tusi explained. "These are adults. Those are the children." He indicated a small group of graves nearby. Black stones traced oval outlines. The shape reminded me of the oval bases of fale; the stones, of fale posts. Deep roots hold Samoans. Most of those who fled Saleʻaula returned within a few years to begin again and link future generations to the ancient land.

I first saw the importance of ceremony with Moelagi Jackson, a ranking female high chief and talking chief, the owner of a hotel, and the widow of a British diplomat. We attended a *kava* ceremony held in my honor in Salimu, a village on the east coast of Savaiʻi.

Moelagi introduced me as "a writer, a tusitala, like Robert Louis Stevenson." The two high chiefs of Salimu hummed approval. Women placed a garland of pink frangipani around my neck and a red hibiscus over my ear. Moelagi and I sat cross-legged on mats in front of fale posts. As the honored guest, I sat at a central post reserved for visiting high chiefs.

In speech after speech the high chiefs' eloquent orators spoke to us. "Welcome, especially you from the higher powers," they began. They presented dried kava plants and recounted kava's traditional importance. Other chiefs supervised the mixing of the pounded roots with water.

Moelagi translated orations, but we remained unaware of an awkward situation. The talking chief who spoke in our behalf was unfamiliar with Robert Louis Stevenson, but assumed he was a person of rank, and did not dare insult me by addressing me by a lower title. In loud, melodious tones he spoke at length of being humbled to be with us, of "this beautiful moment," of the high honor of kava. He ended by turning to me. Suddenly his solution soared beyond the problem, and he boomed, "It is also a joy to act in behalf of you, the President of the United States!"

I accepted the honored first cup of kava, poured a few drops on the mat—by custom once a gift to ancient gods, now an offering to Jehovah—and drank. Kava holds the flavor of earth and forest; it has the taste of roots, the bite of pepper. Samoan gods once spoke through kava orators, and the drink is still treated as a sacred legacy.

Storytelling is only one Polynesian art form preserved by Samoans. Increasingly, youths embrace traditional tattooing as a statement of cultural pride. Forbidden by early missionaries to Polynesia, the custom of extensive tattooing survives only in Samoa. It is a ritual of agony that takes days or even years to complete. "The woman must bear children, the man must be tattooed . . . ," says an old song.

"It means manhood, it shows how brave they are," explained Moelagi. "Any boy or man who chooses can be tattooed. It's good to have it done before you become a matai, because it's very difficult for a matai to say to a young person 'You coward!' when he is a coward himself, with no tattoo."

Moelagi and her brother, matai Leota Viliamu, or Bill, spoke of the blue-black designs that extended from above his waist to below his knees. A canoe with fishing spears decorated his back.

"All the designs mean something in our life," said Bill. "These lines are the beams and ribs of the fale." He traced geometric lines on his back and sides. "And on the thighs, more parts of the house, and these are cone shells." The tattoo ended below his knees in a fringelike pattern. "The tied leaves of thatch on a fale," Bill explained.

"Usually groups of young men are tattooed together," said Moelagi. "Sometimes they ask a chief's daughter to be tattooed as a finale. Women's designs are on the thighs and look like lace. I was asked, but I always refused." She laughed. "Those were the days of the miniskirts."

Song and dance also preserve tradition. Evenings at Moelagi's hotel in Safua village, guests and her children and staff gathered at one end of a giant fale. To the rhythmic strumming of guitars, Moelagi danced the *siva,* her delicate arm and hand movements expressing the Samoan universe—the heavens, the flow of the sea, the flight of a bird. Her white-haired great-uncle, high chief of Safua and bearer of the ancestral title of the god-chief Lealali, joined the young men to perform. Dressed in a rose-colored lava-lava, a flower at his ear, a benevolent smile on his face, he danced with the supple grace of youth.

Children learn history through song. Young men sang of the Mau movement of the 1920s and '30s, when Western Samoans protested New Zealand rule through noncooperation and nonviolence.

One evening the family and staff sang of Tusitala. Even the youngest children joined in as the song began. Alternating Samoan and English verses, it included lines from Stevenson's "Requiem" used as his epitaph:

Here he lies where he longed to be;
Home is the sailor, home from the sea,
And the hunter home from the hill.

Stevenson had aided one matai-led political group as German influence encroached in the late 19th century. In 1900, under an agreement reached by Germany, the United States, and Great Britain, Western Samoa became a German colony and the eastern islands, a U. S. territory. New Zealand took over Western Samoa in 1914 at the outset of World War I, then ruled it as a protectorate under the League of Nations and later the United Nations. In 1962 it became the first Pacific island nation to gain independence. Despite years of foreign rule, the leadership of the matai remained strong.

Of the 47 members of Western Samoa's legislative assembly, 45 are by law matai, and one member, the Honorable Le Tagaloa Pita, holds one of the country's highest matai titles. It can be traced back to the creator god. A leading economist as well, Le Tagaloa Pita spoke to me of fa'a Samoa and Western custom in a modern world.

"Western man's work has been to accumulate and store in times of scarcity," he said. "His attitude has been 'If you do not look after yourself, who will?' Contrast that with the Samoan way: Our challenge has been how to use the relative abundance of nature to make a community livable.

"Matai control 80 percent of the land, but it belongs to everybody. This feeling of community is very strong. There are 162,000 of us here in Western Samoa and at least as many Samoans living overseas. If they come back and trace their family, they find it and they're welcome. They get land. You know, in Samoa it doesn't matter if you're a millionaire; if you haven't shared, nobody cares about you. This is what we see for our future—and the only alternative for the future of the world. If the spirit of sharing isn't put into practice, you'll never have peace.

"That's not saying we're peaceful all the time. We're violent as well—human. Intrigue happens every day, but when the chips are down, people all pull together. We belong to Samoa—to the place and the attitude."

American Samoan leaders echo the same theme as those in Western Samoa: We are one language, one people. In Pago Pago, capital of American Samoa, I visited A. U. Fuimaono, a senator and one of seven paramount chiefs on the island of Tutuila.

"Western Samoans were raised under the influence of Great Britain and Germany. We were raised under the influence of the United States," he pointed out. "That's the difference, but in culture and custom we are the same. I wish very much we could become one Samoa. This is my solution: Develop our economic system among ourselves—share with our neighbors. My strong feeling is it's very wrong to separate us from our brothers." He lowered his eyes and said softly, "We have paradise lost."

To the newly arrived, Tutuila seems paradise *(Continued on page 28)*

Thighs marked with traditional tattoos, Savai'i fisherman Sai Tupai paddles his dugout canoe with outrigger across a lagoon. Wearing goggles and grasping a spear gun, he pursues fish above a bed of coral (below), then returns to his hand-hewn log craft with his catch secure in his mouth.

Youngsters stroll to school in uniforms of blue lavalava, *wraparound skirts commonly worn in Samoa. Formal education, free but not compulsory, lasts only a few years for most Western Samoan children; some go on to vocational school or university. Below, men fish from the brink of a lava flow. Harvesting food from the sea and from inland plantations requires community effort, and entire villages share in nature's bounty.*

Ritual of agony: Tattoo artist Sulu'ape Petelo uses tools of sharpened boars' tusks and dye made of lamp soot to adorn his brother-in-law with age-old designs. Assistants draw the skin taut to receive deep, painful jabs. Samoans continue the ancient Polynesian practice once forbidden by missionaries. Patterns vary little among artists; each element holds special significance related to home and environment. The waist-to-knee design on the man at right may have taken months to complete. Such tattoos prove manhood and show pride of heritage. An old song guarantees the wearer "an everlasting gem that you will take into your grave."

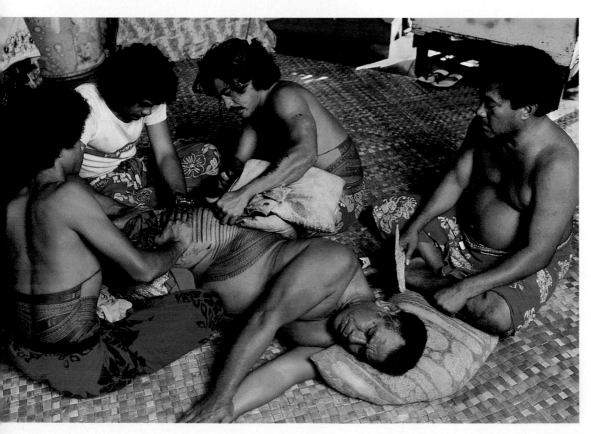

found. It is the largest and most populous of American Samoa's seven inhabited islands. Yachts, ferries, and freighters slash silken wakes across the long, dark blue harbor of Pago Pago. Craggy peaks tangled in tropical foliage rise abruptly from the sea, leaving little level ground for villages and farming plots except along the shore.

Legend says Mount Pioa and Mount Matafao, peaks on either side of the entrance to the bay, were unruly boys whose father turned them to stone for hurling stones at one another. Tradition warns that if clouds form over Mount Pioa—the Rainmaker—a downpour is certain.

A few villages perch on clouded peaks. "Come to church in my village on Sunday and stay to dinner," Senator Fuimaono said. "It's the one closest to God," he added with a smile. A'oloau Fou straddles the long ridge that splits the island. No settlement in American Samoa is loftier.

*T*he booming of a huge slit-log drum summoned worshipers, and I joined them at the church entrance. Most of the women wore white dresses, many of them long, loose-fitting muumuus, a modest style introduced by 19th-century missionaries. Men wore jackets with matching tailored lavalava instead of trousers. We left our shoes outside and then glided past a man in a back pew who shook a whip at the feet of the forgetful and at the startled faces of children not cathedral-quiet. Soon the Samoan sounds of sermon, prayers, and a cappella harmonies of traditional Methodist hymns filled the sanctuary. The choir ended the service softly singing "Hallelujah, *fa'afetai*—Praise, thanks."

Afterward, I met with the council of chiefs in a nearby round fale, its shape traditional for matai meetings. I sat on the floor with Senator, or at that moment Paramount Chief, Fuimaono to dine on taro, yams, and chicken still warm from the ground oven and on corned beef, a requisite at Samoan feasts since the days of the sailing ships.

The council meets each Sunday. "We take care of village business," Chief Fuimaono explained. "We also settle problems the old way—the council decides what to do about a fight, a robbery. It's rare to call in police here. I'm very proud of that." An orator read topics for consideration, while far below silver light glittered on the calm water and on the shore where La Pérouse's men had died almost 200 years ago. Samoans still call it Massacre Bay.

Few roads or even tracks traverse that rugged north shore. Government boats call at isolated villages periodically to drop off supplies and provide transportation. But a paved road extends the length of the south coast, with enough vehicles to cause rush-hour traffic jams morning and afternoon near bayside fish canneries. It is America in miniature. Cars and tiny buses built on pickup-truck beds inch past boutiques, restaurants, and video stores, their radios blaring hit tunes from the States.

Octogenarian Aggie Grey—part Samoan, part Scottish—dances a graceful siva *at her hotel in Apia, where she and her staff often perform for visitors.*

FOLLOWING PAGES: *Pago Pago, American Samoa's capital and main port, bustles with shipping and industry. Island residents elect their own governing officials and send a nonvoting representative to the U. S. Congress.*

I met uniformed Boy Scouts hurrying toward an encampment in a park beside Pago Pago Bay. They clutched brightly fringed mats that would serve as sleeping bags. For a few days some would exchange fale for zippered tent and ground oven for campfire to learn what it's like to rough it in the open air, American style.

Teenagers also gathered in the park to breakdance. Six of them, all related except one, wore high-topped sneakers, dark jackets, and elated smiles—they had recently won the island championship. Named the Famous Original Blood Brothers of Samoa, the group calls itself the Fobbz. "We ran out of esses," one laughed. They have assumed such stateside nicknames as J-Stick, Tickrock, and Casual.

"We learn from movies and video," said another. "We meet to do a little rockin', poppin', invent our own moves." Grinning, they danced in place as we chatted. One "moonwalked" away, then shuffled forward. Another placed cardboard on the grass as a dance platform and with increasing speed gyrated on his hands and shoulders and whirled on his head. They drifted off to challenge another group to top their moves.

The impact of American media and material goods accelerates change and growing differences between the two Samoas. "Other islanders call us

Arms swaying, dancers welcome the British cruise ship Oriana *to Pago Pago. Passengers from several liners disembark here and at other South Pacific islands for daylong visits; many return for lengthy stays. Tourism boosts American Samoa's economy, long dependent on U. S. aid.*

Polyester Polynesians," an American Samoan commented with a mixture of pride and regret. A local proverb expresses the ambivalent feelings of most Samoans in their desire for progress—and their dread of its consequences: Wanting the forest, yet fearing the spirits. Through Western influence and financial aid, the 35,000 people of American Samoa have gained one of the highest standards of living in the South Pacific.

I saw both tradition and cultural change in the family of Barbara and Sau Ueligitone. Barbara grew up in the Midwest, and Sau is native American Samoan; they met in California. Now Barbara works for the Department of Public Health, and Sau is a leading artist.

"Ueligitone is my father's name, the Samoan version of Wellington," Sau explained. "We've taken it as our family name. Having surnames is a recent custom in Samoa."

We served ourselves from an American-style buffet and sat at the dining table in their non-Samoan house of wood and glass.

"There have been adjustments," Barbara conceded. "Obligations of money and time. Right now we're helping pay for a family wedding. Each month brings something new."

Sau was born in Manua, American Samoa's easternmost island group, its history filled with noble heroes and leaders.

"A Samoan family here adopted me," he said. "That's quite common, to have two families. This house is built on my adoptive family's land, but I think of it as ours, not the family's. My Manua family offered me a matai title, but it's such a responsibility. So far I have refused it. I change with the times, but I choose what changes I'll make.

"I teach the boys to cook traditional food in a ground oven. I demand that the children show respect, but I never hit them. Speaking gently but firmly is just as effective."

Barbara cradled a baby girl in her arms. "My sister's," said Sau. "She had too many for her to handle. We wanted another daughter, so when this one was born we asked if we could adopt her." He chuckled. "She said, 'I thought you'd never ask!' "

Sau's paintings show his views of Samoa in transition—the eagle soaring away after dropping a dollar bill, a tattooed child playing in a broken kava bowl. But before the evening ended, Sau mused, "Someday, maybe I'll accept a matai title in Manua—maybe."

My last day on Savai'i, the matai of Safua had summoned me to their meeting. "Lealali," they greeted me, and seated me at the post of a visiting high chief. They had divided the ancient hero-chief title of Moelagi's great-uncle as an honor and bestowed it on me with speeches and kava. Moelagi translated and accepted on my behalf. I promised to return.

I had come as a papalagi to explore paradise, but I found a land with truth more compelling than illusion. I had come as a traveler seeking an exotic, carefree realm and found farsighted chiefs guiding their people into a modern world. I had come as a tusitala, a teller of tales, to write of impressions and glimpses. I found storytellers, poets, singers nurturing their heritage for generations unborn. I discovered Samoans to be eager dispellers of myths not of their making. Yet they remain proud children of Le Tagaloa and willing heirs to a legacy of legend.

Pageantry of the past lingers in Samoa. Women wearing colorful puletasi *present gifts of finely woven mats at the title-granting ceremony of two new high chiefs. The time-honored ritual on Tutuila, American Samoa, brought a thousand visitors from Western Samoa for a day of orations, feasting, dancing, and singing. By custom in both countries, a new chief serves on his village council and may rise to the rank of paramount chief. Although politically divided, the two Samoas remain united through bonds of kinship, sharing one culture and one language.*

TONGA

Polynesia's Last Kingdom

By Gene S. Stuart
Photographs by David Hiser

When ancient Tongans dreamed of paradise, they imagined a distant island of natural perfection filled with fragrant flowers, succulent fruits, and abundant hogs.

When modern foreigners fantasize a tropical heaven on earth, they might be imagining Tonga: islands with a climate neither cold nor too hot; a peaceable kingdom whose monarch rules from an elegant palace beside the sea; a realm that has been called a gigantic garden, where it is written that every young man shall be given land to cultivate and to build a home. Dream of a country where singing and dancing, feasting and giving gifts are among the most important things in life. Such a place exists. Such a life is real. The people smile and say, "It is *faka-Tonga,* the Tonga way."

The country's setting seems no less magical. The islands border the Tonga Trench. At more than 35,000 feet below sea level, the fissure is the deepest in the South Pacific. Imagine the ocean without water: Tonga's islands would be among earth's loftiest peaks. Let the water return, and pretend that Hawaii's Mauna Kea, the world's tallest mountain, has been lowered into the Tonga Trench. Measuring some 32,000 feet from seafloor to summit, it would lie 3,000 feet below the ocean's surface.

According to Tongan legend, the earth rests on a goddess, Havea Hikule'o. When she moves, the earth quakes. A 19th-century English observer noted, "on such occasions, the people give loud shouts, and beat the ground with sticks," which supposedly makes the goddess lie still.

One Tongan creation legend says that the Polynesian god Maui hoisted the islands from the ocean floor with a fishhook. He stepped on some to flatten them for gardens. They are the coral islands. Soaring cones mark those he left untrodden. They are the volcanic islands.

Horse-drawn cart with colt alongside carries villagers to farm plots on Tongatapu Island. Such conveyances remain a common sight in rural areas. PRECEDING PAGES: *Sunset heightens the tranquillity of Port of Refuge in the Vava'u island group. Named by a Spanish commander in 1781, these waters once harbored Tongan voyaging canoes and now shelter far-ranging yachts.*

FLOWER ART: TORCH GINGER *(Nicolaia elatior)*

Maui's realm is divided into three main island groups: Tongatapu, Ha'a-pai, and Vava'u. A small group, the Niua, lies so far north of the others that many maps do not include it. Strewn across thousands of square miles of ocean, Tonga's 150 or more islands total only about 270 square miles.

After the islands' creation, lush forests grew and were filled with exotic birds. Coconut trees edged white sandy shores. Protective reefs formed, and tropical fish flitted among bright blossoms of coral. Then from out of the west across the blue sea came the precursors of the Tongan kings.

Scholars believe these ancestors arrived from islands in Southeast Asia by way of Melanesia. Radiocarbon dating of Lapita pottery, a type made by pre-Polynesian peoples, places settlers in Fiji by 1250 B.C. Tentative dates indicate some occupied Tongatapu by 1140 B.C., and others were living in Samoa two centuries later.

Most experts view the migrations as planned voyages rather than accidental ones. Having found these unoccupied islands, whether by exploration or happenstance, people often returned to populated ones to spread news of discovery. In later centuries they ranged outward, usually from Samoa, to settle eastern Polynesia. By A.D. 850 they occupied the Society Islands and Hawaii, and by 1000, New Zealand and the Cook Islands. Polynesia was the last large habitable region on earth to be populated.

Consider the achievement of the ancient navigators in finding these far-flung islands, insignificant specks in the world's largest ocean. It seems impossible at first glance. But an expert on Polynesian navigation, David Lewis, notes that it is possible to sail from Southeast Asia to all the inhabited islands of Oceania, except Hawaii, New Zealand, and Easter Island, without ever making a sea crossing longer than 310 nautical miles. Samoa lies only 162 miles beyond Tonga's Niua Islands, and Fiji's easternmost group is about 188 miles from Tongatapu. During his late 18th-century visits, Capt. James Cook estimated that some oceangoing canoes could travel 120 miles or more a day. Tongan canoes carried dozens of people and their supplies. By day, navigators read such signs as ocean swells, currents, winds, and cloud formations. At night they read the stars as well.

Through the centuries the islanders of Samoa, Fiji, and Tonga kept in close contact. The purposes of their visits ranged from trade to warfare to intermarriage among ruling families.

Western Samoan oral tradition tells of a navigational mishap and subsequent intrigue among inter-island elite. I had heard the story from my friend Moelagi Jackson on the Samoan island of Savai'i. The mishap occurred around 1545 and gave rise to one of her chiefly titles, Va'asiliifiti.

"Tongan boats called at the springs here in the village of Safua for fresh water," she began. "The Tongans noticed that the chief of Safua had handsome sons. They went back to Tonga with the news. The daughter of the Tu'i Tonga, the king, came to Safua and married one of the sons, Tupa'i.

"When she was going to have a baby, she told the chief of Safua that she should have it in Tonga so it would become the heir of the Tu'i Tonga. The couple took off in a boat, but the navigators didn't do their job well. Currents carried them toward Fiji. They could see Fiji there, and she was due and became upset. 'What the hell happened?' she said. 'We're not in Tonga and I'm having the baby!' He was born in the boat. She named the child

Va'asiliifiti—Boat-That-Overran-to-Fiji. Tupa'i was afraid, because at that time there was trouble between Samoa and Fiji. He told his wife to tell the Fijians he was her brother. She did and then married the son of the King of Fiji. Tupa'i married a Fijian woman, but later he came back to Samoa, bringing his son Va'asiliifiti with him. This happened about 15 generations ago—family history."

The Tu'i Tonga line of kings ruled Tonga for nine centuries, beginning about A.D. 950. Tradition says the first monarch was the son of a god and a woman from Tongatapu. In the 13th century a Tu'i Tonga gave a title and temporal power to his brother. Later, a member of that dynasty created a third line in the same way. By the time of Captain Cook's visits, power had been dispersed among the chiefs. The Tu'i Tonga remained a sacred figurehead of high rank but little authority. The last holder of the title, the 38th in the long dynastic line, died in 1865.

Nuku'alofa, Tonga's tranquil little capital, edges a wide bay on the northern coast of Tongatapu. Wharves stretch toward low offshore islands. Architecture reflects history: Victorian cottages screened by hibiscus, poinsettia, and frangipani recall British influence after Wesleyan missionaries settled there in the 1800s.

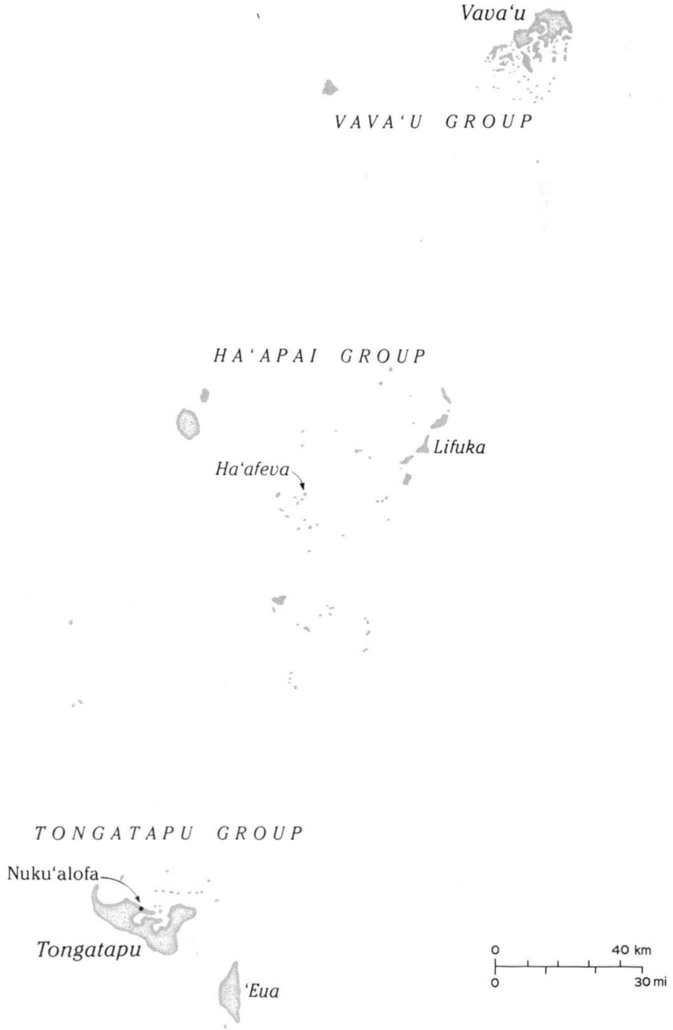

Scattered realm of some 150 islands—fewer than 40 of them inhabited—spans 400 miles from north to south. A total land area of just 270 square miles makes the Kingdom of Tonga smaller than New York City. Only the main island groups shown here appear on most maps of the country; other isles—the Niua—lie many miles to the north. Tonga placed itself under the protection of Great Britain in 1900, but regained independence in 1970.

Vava'u

VAVA'U GROUP

HA'APAI GROUP

Lifuka

Ha'afeva

TONGATAPU GROUP

Nuku'alofa

Tongatapu

'Eua

0   40 km

0   30 mi

In the large sitting room of one such house, I met Mrs. ʻOtoʻota ʻEva, a member of Langa Fonua, a women's handicraft cooperative founded by the late Queen Sālote. The house serves as the handicraft shop, and baskets, trays, mats, and tapa cloth filled many rooms. Mrs. ʻEva showed me how to put a design on a panel of tapa, or mulberry-bark cloth. She stretched some tapa across a stencil made of coconut fiber and coconut-leaf ribs. Then she rubbed the cloth with a wad of dye-dipped tapa, and I watched the design emerge.

"Tapa is an important tradition—a gift at births, christenings, weddings, and funerals," she said. It is of such importance that Tongans even see shadows on the full moon as a woman beating strips of bark into cloth for her daughter's wedding as the girl looks on.

Mrs. ʻEva also introduced me to a striking Tongan custom. She picked up a handwoven mat the size of a small carpet, wrapped it around herself, and tied it with a rope. It reached from armpit to ankle.

"My family is in mourning for an auntie, so I don't go outside without my large mat," she explained. "We have other mats for everyday wear."

We toured the town, and in the streets I saw that most men and women, young and old, wore mats of various sizes. Some women wore belts with dangling panels instead. Materials varied from coconut fiber to plastic thread. One matron swept past in a swirl of old cassette tapes that rustled to her knees.

"In wearing these mats and belts, we express our respect for each other and for the royal family," said Mrs. ʻEva.

A drive out of town took me through plantations of coconut, banana, taro, and yams, and villages bright with carefully groomed grass and flowers. A sign painted on the mat wall of a backyard animal pen instructed: GO FOR IT. Pigs did, uprooting a circle of rich soil in a perfect lawn while excited chickens went for morsels unearthed by the trotters. Exploring narrow, sandy roads, I came upon horse-drawn two-wheeled carts laden with fruits and vegetables. Tongans are so polite that everyone stops to let everyone else pass, creating a gridlock of grinning inertia. Faka-Tonga.

I visited sites Tongans show with pride: the Haʻamonga trilithon, a massive stone structure erected about A.D. 1200 by the 11th Tuʻi Tonga; stone-faced earthen tombs of the ancient kings; coral blowholes that spew water a hundred feet into the air at high tide.

At Kolovai, near Tongatapu's northwestern tip, hundreds of fruit bats hang like pods from lofty casuarina trees by day. Called flying foxes because of their golden fur and pointed ears, they folded their black leathery wings and settled in to rest as I watched one Sunday morning. Bat disputes over hanging spaces filled the air with shrill squeaks. Some bats took wing, circled, and glided back to a branch. One, shoved to exasperation but unwilling to move, threw an inverted tantrum. The squeaking din blended with hymns from a church across the road, and the sounds rose heavenward in unison. By tradition the flying foxes of Kolovai are sacred. Centuries ago, a Samoan princess, enamored of a Tongan navigator, gave the first Kolovai bats to him as tokens of her love. Many Pacific islanders consider bats a delicacy, but only members of Tonga's royal family are permitted to shoot the ones at Kolovai.

A brilliant 19th-century chief of royal lineage, Taufa'ahau, reunited Tonga after he seized power from all other chiefs; took a concubine of the Tu'i Tonga as his own; made peace with Fiji; persuaded the chiefs who remained heathen to accept Christianity; and even converted the King of Fiji. As King George Tupou I, he gave Tonga a constitution and a nobility.

One of the nation's 33 hereditary nobles, the Honorable Ve'ehala, served as governor of Ha'apai for nearly 17 years before his retirement in 1984. He spoke proudly of Tongan history and of King George I, whose great-great-granddaughter, beloved Queen Sālote Tupou III, was the mother of the present monarch, King Taufa'ahau Tupou IV. He spoke affectionately of things dear to Tongan hearts—of sea voyages and stars.

"How Tongans travel! The sea is part of their life. Family branches are scattered around these islands. Tongans want to see their relatives, and they like to travel. A few years back, when I was a boy, there were only cutters with sails, no engines. They could float for six or seven days between Ha'apai and Tongatapu if there was dead calm. I went by cutter—enjoyed it so many times. People used to go up to the Niua, to Samoa and Fiji.

Enfolded in tradition, the Honorable Ve'ehala, one of Tonga's 33 nobles, and his wife wear ta'ovala—*finely woven pandanus-leaf mats. Over generations, many titled members of Ve'ehala's family have owned his ceremonial mat. Samoans wove his wife's treasured heirloom, said to be 500 years old.*

FOLLOWING PAGES: *Mounds of melons and other produce in the market at Nuku'alofa, the capital, attest bountiful crops in an agricultural economy.*

"Her late majesty, Queen Sālote, took the Methodist Church cutter from Nuku'alofa to Suva, Fiji, to catch a mail boat to Australia in the 1930s. That old cutter used to be the biggest boat in Tonga—a 40-footer. I went with her on it to Ha'apai and Vava'u, then on to the Niua. Oh, the Queen was not a good sailor, but when she had to sail she seemed to enjoy it. Her captain was from a well-known Tongan family of navigators. He and his crew of two took turns with the rudder. When they traveled in Tonga, they covered the compass—the crew could hardly read it—and took it down below in case a wave hit the boat and the compass went overboard. They never ran aground. They just steered by instinct and the stars.

"Each star had a name. For some stars, navigators looked to the horizon. An old head navigator might say to a young one, 'When that star starts to come up, another will take its place. If you're traveling north, yes, follow that star. Now it starts to go west. But you have your new star. There it is! Follow that. By daylight you'll see the morning star come out. Then we'll be at such and such a place.'

"I was listening to the broadcast of shipping traffic the other night: 'A boat is traveling from Tonga to Pago Pago, Apia, Tarawa, Port Moresby. Another is coming here by way of Christmas Island.' And I thought: All Tongan captains. They roam the Pacific."

One afternoon near sunset I boarded the broad, flat-bottomed ferry *Olovaha* at Nuku'alofa to roam northward through the Ha'apai island group to Vava'u. Almost all the passengers were Tongan. They clustered on the wharf saying tearful farewells to friends and relatives. One group harmonized a hymn with a minister. He prayed and blessed the voyage, and we inched like willing Jonahs into the great maw of the flat-faced prow that lay open to receive cargo and passengers.

Tongans staked claims on deck space, unrolled sleeping mats, and opened large boxes of food. "I'm seasick," moaned one man. The bay was as smooth as a mirror. My tiny cabin held bunk beds, a table, a sea-stained bench, and a locker—locked. "Don't open the porthole. The sea will come in," the steward warned.

When we reached the churning open sea, I did and it did. The ferry climbed waves, hovered on crests with propellers screaming in air, then scurried down into troughs. Without a deep keel, it slid from side to side as well. Across the passageway in the crew's galley, the cooks' shrieking laughter increased in direct ratio to the crash of crockery and the clang of falling metal trays and pans. On deck, Tongans donned knitted caps and jackets against the balmy night and settled in to joke and feast, faka-Tonga.

A group of young Australians, volunteers in a service similar to the American Peace Corps, sipped sodas and talked excitedly of their mission to Ha'apai and the blessings it would bring—the installation of water pumps and pipes. Soulful German youths in shorts and sturdy boots sat apart and spoke to no one. They spread multiple slices of dark bread with peanut butter and dutifully swallowed them, and stoically stared out to sea as if South Pacific travel were an obligatory rite of passage.

Before dawn the sea calmed in the shelter of the Ha'apai group, and crew members in the galley prayed and sang hymns. We anchored outside the reef of small, low Ha'afeva Island while shouting, laughing passengers filled small launches until they rode perilously low in the water. The ferry crew played spotlights on the narrow passage through the reef and saw the boats safely to shore.

As a young officer, William Bligh had accompanied Captain Cook on his third Pacific voyage, from 1777 to 1780, and visited Ha'apai. In 1789 Bligh returned to the Pacific in command of the *Bounty*. Mutineers, wishing to return to the easy life and beautiful women of Tahiti, set him and 18 of his crew adrift in an open boat near Ha'afeva. Kept from landing in Fiji by hostile natives, Bligh and his men voyaged more than 3,600 nautical miles before reaching the East Indies.

At first light we sailed among low coral islands and past the distant blue-gray cone of Kao. Soon after sunrise the *Olovaha* stopped at Lifuka, another of the god Maui's flat gardens, where a Victorian house that serves as a summer palace dominates a row of wooden bungalows and shoreline palm trees. Cook visited this coral island on his third voyage, and a powerful chief, Finau I, dined aboard his ship. On shore, Finau entertained the visitors with feasting, dancing, and athletic contests. Cook named the isles he saw the Friendly Islands, unaware of a Tongan plot to murder him and plunder his ships. Unable to agree among themselves, the conspirators abandoned the plan.

Some 30 years later at Lifuka, another chief, Finau II, captured a private warship, the *Port au Prince,* and killed most of the crew. Finau adopted one survivor, 15-year-old William Mariner, assuming the English youth to be, Mariner recalled, "a young chief of some consequence. . . ." Finau, a group of his men, and the survivors took the ship "Through a very narrow passage, so full of rocks and shoals as to appear unnavigable. . . . She was brought within half a cable's length of the shore, and run aground by Finow's directions." The chief ordered the guns removed for use in wars, and the ship plundered for metal and then burned.

Cables bound the *Olovaha* to the wharf at Lifuka while workers off-loaded lumber, dried pandanus leaves used in basketry, and barrels of petroleum. Such cargo would have puzzled Finau. After Mariner explained the use of coins, the chief commented, "I had always thought your ship belonged to some poor fellow, perhaps to King George's cook; for Captain Cook's ship, which belonged to the King, had plenty of beads, axes and looking-glasses on board, whilst yours had nothing but iron hoops, oil, skins and twelve thousand *pa'anga*. . . ." Finau had mistaken silver pieces of eight for pa'anga—gaming pieces.

Casting off in midafternoon, the *Olovaha* maneuvered through rocks and shoals as the *Port au Prince* had done—a passage the ferry captain prefers to make in daylight, because, said a crew member, "It's too dangerous and tricky at night."

After dark, black heavens gradually filled with brilliant stars, and either the sea had become choppier or the ferry's lightened load increased the craft's tendency to bob and slide. Although we steered a steady course, the *Olovaha* seemed to speed first toward one star, then toward another. Along passageways, on decks, and over the side, Tongans by the score proved that although they are enthusiastic travelers, they are poor sailors.

Before midnight the sea calmed as we slipped into the Vava'u group. We picked our way through a long passage by playing spotlights along island shores. After 29 hours on the ferry, travelers lined the rails and watched,

thankful for a safe journey. It was probably not by coincidence that most worshipers of the ancient gods of voyages and canoes lived in Vava'u. At the end of the passage twinkled the lights of Neiafu, a town perched above a harbor whose name I praised—Port of Refuge.

Tongans lovingly refer to the hilly, raised coral islands of Vava'u as mountainous and proudly call the harbor one of the most beautiful in the Pacific. I would agree. The islands are also among the most bountiful.

A recently arrived foreigner was amazed to see twigs he used for tomato stakes sprout and grow as fast as the tomato plants themselves. When I toured an experimental government plantation, I noted that stakes of *fiki*—fig—supporting vanilla plants had done the same, their leaves providing shade. Vanilla has become the leading cash crop in Tonga. Each acre yields about a hundred pounds of cured pods, or beans. Tonga ships tons of the beans to the United States annually. But there is trouble in paradise. The Tongan population, 77,400 in 1966, has climbed to nearly 100,000. A young man cannot expect the 8-acre plot promised by the constitution.

"Only if he's an heir," the Honorable Ve'ehala had told me. "But we still can manage. People are fed and there's no hunger. And the number emigrating legally and illegally—there are about 30,000 Tongans overseas—keeps the population down, and they send back money.

"Families who have no land do survive. They ask a friend or a relative, 'Can we go to your allotment and plant a few tapioca and bananas for ourselves?' 'Why not,' they are told. Or sometimes the owner works in an

Modern artisans practice the ancient craft of making tapa cloth from the inner bark of paper mulberry trees. After joining sections into a 63-foot length (opposite), women apply dark vegetable dye to stenciled designs. Rites of passage from birth to death require gifts of tapa. Long pieces often become "red carpets" for royalty or newlyweds. Before Europeans introduced woven fabric, tapa served many uses—from mosquito netting to clothing. At right, speedy fingers fashion a basket from dried pandanus leaves and coconut-leaf ribs. This cottage industry, geared to the tourist trade, supplements family income.

Preacher Leveni Tuʻitupou Faingataʻa delivers an emphatic sermon, and the congregation harmonizes a hymn at a Wesleyan Methodist church on Vavaʻu. Sunday worshipers attend morning and afternoon services, breaking for midday feasts. Strict laws prohibit Sabbath work or travel; even airlines cannot operate. Choirs practice for services or singing contests several nights a week. In 1834 British Wesleyan missionaries converted the King of Tonga to Christianity; his nation soon followed, and today nearly half the country's 100,000 people are Methodists.

office. He says, 'I have no time to cultivate. You cultivate for us.' It's exchanging. Sharing is common. Whole villages send plates of food to that neighbor and that neighbor on Sundays. They in turn subdivide it for that cousin and that cousin. When my wife and I have a piece of pork or something, we think, 'Let's give some to our friends and neighbors.' And our priest always gets his share. Piles of food are distributed, and everyone will return every kindness shown him. We don't have any welfare at all."

Kilino Patolo and his two brothers share a 20-acre allotment on the Niua island of Tafahi, the 2,000-foot cone of an extinct volcano. Kilino's tall, athletic build is typically Tongan, and so is his expansive smile. The brothers grow Tonga's second most profitable cash crop, *kava.*

"Best kava in Tonga. It's smooth and strong," Kilino said. "We use no fertilizer. The soil is so rich we grow a thousand kava plants to an acre and get twenty dollars a plant. But then the land must lie fallow at least three years. About 400 people live on Tafahi. It's different from the rest of Tonga—hot and humid. The mountain is so fertile—volcanic soil keeps washing down—even the steep slopes are cultivated. Many people climb to 75 degrees, both angle and temperature, to plant crops." He planned to marry his American girlfriend and move to Maryland. He smiled: "If Maryland doesn't work out, we can always go back to Tafahi and grow kava."

Boyhood excitement for Kilino was crossing a treacherous channel in a small boat to reach a nearby island, or glimpsing Tafahi's pale hermit, Tavi, climbing on the mountain slopes outside his hut.

Tavi now lives in Tongatapu, where I met him. He was thin, delicate, and he wore a straw hat large enough to serve as shelter. Gray-blue eyes shone from his ascetic face. I learned how Preben Kauffmann, from a Danish noble family, had become Tavi.

"After the atomic bomb I expected the Third World War. I was an engineer, but my mother wanted me to be an architect. Instead of improving the world, I thought I might as well improve myself. I chose Tonga and a new name after doing research in a library, and came here in 1952 and some years later to Tafahi to live on the cone. People thought I was a spy; *papalangi*—foreigners—are suspect. But the royal family believed in me, and I told the King I wanted to stay. The present Queen adopted me. I can't be Tongan in my heart, but I am free of most of my Danish heritage."

Tavi has designed a house for the royal princess. An astute scholar, he helped edit an account of Tongan society at the time of Cook's visits, based largely on interviews with Queen Sālote. A keen observer, he understands modern Tongans and their complex traditions.

"Not so long ago, Tongans believed in devils but not in germs," he said. "Most believed diseases came through ghosts. Land, marriage, funerals—it's all tied up with spirits. In the old days the chief's eldest sister controlled them. The whole system starts with brothers and sisters. A sister has higher rank, but a brother has more power. The sister is higher because she has

Passengers board the inter-island ferry Olovaha *at Nuku'alofa for a journey northward. Ancient Tongans explored the South Pacific in large canoes; their descendants go voyaging to visit friends and relatives on distant islands.*

FOLLOWING PAGES: *Golden dawn finds an islander gathering his catch at low tide in Nuku'alofa harbor. Night's incoming tide filled the net with fish.*

a hook in her father's heart. Fathers love their daughters, mothers love their sons. But the husband has his thumb on his wife and therefore on the sons. Children go to their mother's relatives, who are obliged to give them what they want. They avoid their father's relatives because they are obligated to give to them. The important thing is to manipulate and control. It is hard for a family to tear loose from this. Tradition is being diluted by foreign influence and money, but there are still age-old prerogatives.

"The Samoan social system is a truncated pyramid with paramount chiefs at the top. The Tongan system has been more refined. It goes straight up to the gods.

"Tongans have a superficial happy-go-lucky attitude and great humor," said Tavi, laughing. "They enjoy being the butt of a joke. That's a similarity to the Danes, along with their fondness for food."

It is an attitude that is easy to adopt—so easy that I laughed when the dugout canoe I was in began to sink in Vava'u's Port of Refuge harbor.

I had watched the canoes, those craft of ancient heritage, move between the hills that are actually high mountain peaks and across the deep water that fills the valley. Kilifi, a young man from the island of Pangaimotu, offered me a ride in his two-foot-wide dugout. As he paddled us toward his village, water rose around my feet. "There's a two-story house someone built who was overseas," Kilifi said. I jammed a heel into a crack in the hollowed-out log, trying to stop the flow. "And there's our church," he said, pointing with a paddle. Not daring to look up, I bailed frantically with a coconut shell and nodded. By the time our tour ended, I had enjoyed a shoreline view downward into another realm—one of bright fish and coral beneath the water's surface.

I exchanged tradition for luxury. One morning, Lualala Mataele, or Lua, hoisted the mainsail of the 37-foot yacht *Fleur de Lys,* and we slipped southward from Neiafu down the long passage. Lua, a Tongan captain, told me the lore of the islands. We passed flat-topped Mount Talau, which dominates the landscape of Vava'u. A Samoan demon-god had ripped off its summit and hurled it into the bay, creating an island. A Tongan demon-god frightened him away before he could make more geologic mischief. Lua pointed out Mala Island and its deep, treacherous channel. "A cannibal demon-god captured people who dared go near," he said with a smile.

At midday we anchored off the uninhabited island of 'Euakafa. Tides had scattered a bounty of shells on the sandy beach near a coral outcrop where ancient Tongans quarried slabs. I soon saw their purpose. We climbed a lofty hill, through thick tropical growth, until we reached a deep, slab-lined tomb. Lua recounted the tragedy behind its creation as we gazed out on a panorama of emerald islands in a silver sea.

"The 29th Tu'i Tonga, Tele'a, chose to live here with his favorite wife, Talafaiva, because of the view. A *fo'ui* tree hung over the fence around their compound. Talafaiva wanted it cut down, but Tele'a said, 'Leave it.' One night while he was on a fishing trip, a handsome man climbed the tree, came in, and seduced Talafaiva. Tele'a was furious, but his wife said, 'It was because of the tree.' He told a servant to punish her, but the servant killed her instead, and Tele'a had this tomb built. He loved her so much, they say he sat here and cried for days. All that happened hundreds of years ago. Now when we Tongans want to deny responsibility, we joke and say, 'It wasn't my fault, it was the fo'ui tree.' "

As we made our way back to Neiafu, Lua told me of his Pacific adventures. He had worked in a New Zealand factory, fished the seas off Pago Pago. "But I always came back. My daughter wanted to live with relatives in Los Angeles. I said, 'It's up to you.' My son wants to go to a university in the States. I said, 'It's up to you.' Me, I'll stay here. This is my island, this is my home. I'm loyal to Tonga and the Methodist Church. It's the church of the King. If it suits him, it suits me."

In the late afternoon we hove to, and in a dinghy we entered Swallows Cave, with its opalesque stalactites, deep blue water, and schools of electric-blue fish that turned as one with every movement of the boat. Birds' nests dotted the ceiling, and graffiti dating back to the days of whaling ships decorated the walls. A pull on an oar created haunting echoes like the ominous threats of deep-voiced demon-gods.

I had my fill of ocean voyaging and flew back to Tongatapu. Late one night, as I prepared to leave Tonga for Fiji, the hotel began to shake. The earth trembled as if the goddess Hikule'o were trying to shift her heavy burden of earth. Tremors are common in Tonga, but this one was the strongest in years. We swayed from side to side as if we were on an island ship in a stormy sea. Below, from lounge and lobby, rose a chorus of laughter, cheers, and shouts. Tongans bade the goddess rest, and she settled once more into quiet repose. Above, bright stars beckoned to wanderers, and the woman in the moon bent to her tapa. Faka-Tonga.

Palace pet, a Madagascar tortoise roams royal lawns in Nuku'alofa. Presented to the royal family by the National Geographic Society in the 1960s, it took the place of one supposedly given by Capt. James Cook to a powerful chief two centuries ago. The Victorian palace and chapel, completed in 1882, reflect years of British influence. Today Tonga remains a member of the British Commonwealth. The present monarch, Taufa'ahau Tupou IV, traces his regal lineage back a thousand years, and rules the last of Polynesia's great island kingdoms.

*Food and flowers welcome visitors to a sunny beach on cruise-ship days.
Tongans entertain in traditional style with a pig cooked to a turn over an
open fire. Tourists watch a man remove tubers roasted on white-hot stones
in an 'umu, or ground oven, which he covered with banana leaves and a
layer of sand. After two hours of singing and dancing to guitars, foreign
guests and native hosts will now share an age-old custom—a Tongan feast.*

FIJI

South Sea Crossroads

By Gene S. Stuart
Photographs by David Hiser

*E*xcept for the strange sound of it, the incoming tide seemed like others a calm Pacific Ocean sends against the shores of Suva Harbor in Fiji. The flow rose gently, almost imperceptibly, along a seawall that borders wide lawns at the water's edge. But on that Sunday in September, a hissing sound like driving sleet made residents and visitors alike turn in questioning alarm and hurry toward the wall. The sight beyond it stopped us, took our breath away. We stared in silence at a tide of undulating stone.

A brown-gray layer of pumice covered the bright blue sea. Small waves coursed beneath the stones on the water's surface, moving faster than their burden. The floating pumice washed to and fro, inching forward with each surge, then sliding back again. The tidal force increased, and waves in the harbor rose higher to crest, curl forward in rigid plumes, break, then fold down upon themselves, spilling avalanches of brittle spume into churning, gravelly troughs. And the sound of crashing stone, of liquid rockfall, drowned out the crisp clatter of palm fronds and the shrill cries of mynah birds that flitted among them.

"Four to six weeks ago an undersea volcano between Fiji and Tonga erupted," someone said. "Pumice rose to the surface and drifted here with the currents. It has happened before. Sometimes these tides clog bays for days. Copra freighters can't call at islands for a while. We just wait for the stones to wash ashore or be swept away."

A few weeks before, I had felt Tonga shudder from seismic shock. Now stones born of a mountain beneath the sea were drifting to land on Fiji. I wondered if they were manifestations of the same violent event.

Stone and sea, solid and liquid—opposites like these came to symbolize Fiji for me. With its unexpected extremes of nature, its unlikely mixes of

Moistened by Pacific trade winds, a rain forest flourishes in the rugged interior of Viti Levu—Great Fiji—the country's largest island.
PRECEDING PAGES: *Sailboats ride at anchor in the Blue Lagoon in the Yasawa Islands. In 1789 cannibals in war canoes pursued Captain Bligh of the* Bounty *through these waters, now frequented by cruise ships.*

FLOWER ART: SKY VINE *(Thunbergia grandiflora)*

63

peoples, its astonishing twists of history, Fiji is truly a nation of contrasts.

The easternmost islands are small and usually formed of coral; the larger western ones are volcanic. Together they number more than 300, along with several hundred islets, but only a hundred are inhabited. The date line jogs to the east of the islands so that all of Fiji can observe the date in the Eastern Hemisphere. Otherwise, it would be a nation divided between yesterday and today.

More than half of Fiji's nearly 700,000 people live on the largest island, Viti Levu—Great Fiji. Thick foliage blankets its windward side. Halfway across its 100-mile-wide expanse, tropical flora gives way to the sparse trees, wild grasses, and fields of sugarcane that mark the leeward side.

Suva, the capital, has a population of some 70,000, making it the largest city in the South Pacific east of New Zealand. It spreads upward from Suva Harbor across a peninsula of verdant hills. On the outskirts, a few thatch-roofed *bure,* traditional houses, recall the ancient village that once nestled beside the shore. New residential suburbs and industrial buildings attest recent growth. The tree-shaded campus of the University of the South Pacific confirms Fiji's role as an inter-island center for higher education. In brightly flowered gardens, red or yellow flags flutter from swaying bamboo poles, proclaiming the house occupants to be devout Hindus. Closer in, tourist hotels and apartment houses dot the steep skyline. Hills flatten to level ground near the water, where older buildings—wooden chapels in Gothic Revival style and wooden cottages with gingerbread ornament— evoke colonial times.

And on the Sunday that the stone tide rolled in, Fijians dressed in proper whites sedately rolled dark balls on smooth bowling greens in an echo of the old British Empire.

*T*he first known European to view Fiji was Dutch explorer Abel Tasman, who sailed through the islands in 1643. Tales of tangled reefs and savage cannibals discouraged early travelers, but by the mid-19th century the islands had a number of adventurous foreign-born residents: castaways, traders, romantics, criminals, misfits, missionaries, and lunatics, some highly qualified in more than one category.

The native people they found were a complex racial and cultural blend of Melanesian and Polynesian, for Fiji lies along the border scholars define between the two cultural groups. Fierce natives were not unknown to foreigners in the South Pacific, but in Fiji contrasts between European and South Sea customs reached new extremes. In 1840 an American naval officer, Charles Wilkes, called Fijians "the most barbarous and savage race now existing upon the globe." English missionary Thomas Williams wrote: "Atrocities of the most fearful kind have come to my knowledge, which I *dare* not record here." However, he considered grisly tortures and the drinking of human blood and the eating of human flesh to be acceptable subjects and described them in detail. Outsiders, he said, regarded Fijian history as "a scandal to humanity."

Fijians, on the other hand, complained that escaped English criminals living among them were "men of the most desperate wickedness, being regarded as monsters. . . ." They also noted that white monsters, unlike native chiefs, were not divine and had black teeth and bad manners.

Scandalous or not, Fijian history claims roots older than those in Polynesian islands. Voyaging east from the New Hebrides, a people now referred to as the Lapita arrived in Fiji more than 3,000 years ago. Lapita pottery discovered on Viti Levu dates from about 1250 B.C. Early voyagers spread Lapita-style pottery to Tonga, Samoa, and other Pacific islands. Although pottery is no longer made in Tonga and Samoa, it is a thriving cottage industry in the Rewa Delta east of Suva.

Delta travel has changed little over the years. There are few roads; travelers usually walk native tracks or board a motorized punt, as I did, to reach isolated villages. The punt quickly filled with bundle-bearing Fijians returning from visits or shopping expeditions. A large, laughing woman, well prepared for travel in the tropics, opened an expansive umbrella emblazoned "Qantas" as our voyage down the wide Nasilai River began. Under an unforgiving sun, we passed fields of grain, tapioca, and taro, lush pastures, and dark tangles of forest and mangrove. When we stopped at settlements, children called greetings or jumped into the river to frolic like dolphins. My guide, a carefree, joking man named Livai Roruru, was also returning home. He pointed out houses of relatives and shouted to friends.

One bend away from the sea, we stopped at the village of Nasilai, where women dig brown clay from the riverbank and make pottery in the manner of their ancestors: shaped not on a wheel but with paddles; impressed with old designs by sticks, shells, and husks; burnished with stones; and glazed while still hot from the fire with the gum of the *dakua* tree.

Livai guided me along a narrow track and across stream-spanning logs to a nearby settlement—and the house of his mother. We sat on layers of soft mats in the dark bure. Livai's mother and niece sat at the kitchen end and cooked over a small fire. They gave me nods and friendly smiles and offered perfumed coconut oil for anointment. And I recalled that even

Volcanoes and coral reefs helped build most of the 300-odd islands in the Fiji group, a hundred of which are inhabited. The population of 675,000 reflects a mix of cultures in a nation where Melanesia and Polynesia meet.

YASAWA GROUP

Vanua Levu

Taveuni

Ovalau
Levuka
Bau

Viti Levu

Suva

LAU GROUP

0 20 40 60 km

0   20   40 mi

Kadavu

missionary Williams had praised the Fijians' "general kindness of manner" and "politeness and good breeding."

As we made our way back to the landing, Livai gestured in a wide arc and exclaimed, "Here we have fish from the river, just pull them up! We have food from the trees, all you have to do is pick it. Even medicine." He tore leaves from a mile-a-minute plant, a fast-growing vine, and squeezed out the green juice. "Put this on a cut. It stops the flow of blood. We use what nature gives. Our attitude is: Without money we can still live. Let tomorrow come, we'll solve whatever it brings."

In Suva a young female guide had told me, "Americans worry too much. Don't worry. You want a crisis? Worry about time. You'll have a crisis! People in Fiji don't worry about time. We have all our time to take it easy."

But the ethic of hard work had been forced upon Fijian laborers in the early 1800s, when traders began to call, seeking, said Williams, "sandalwood to burn before Chinese idols, or bêche-de-mer [a kind of sea slug] to gratify the palate of Chinese epicures." In return for their subjects' labor, despotic Fijian rulers sought British and American aid in their chiefly rivalries, as well as foreign goods such as firearms and well-appointed schooners. Some chiefs sold vast tracts of land for a pittance.

By 1871 some 3,000 whites had settled in the islands. Many established plantations, but about one-third of them lived in Levuka, then Fiji's capital, a rowdy, filthy town built on a strip of shore at the foot of sheer mountains. Half the buildings were taverns. Ships' captains reputedly found their way into port by following the path of empty bottles that poured out through the reef's narrow opening with each ebb tide. "Swilling gin and brawling are the principal amusements," said a barrister. The newspaper complained that some citizens were "perfect madmen and fit inmates for a lockup. . . ." and that "one of the nuisances of Levuka is the constant report of firearms which lasts almost without intermission day and night. . . ."

Levuka had nowhere to grow and a better port was needed, so in 1882 the capital was moved to Suva, a change the newspaper complained would make Levuka "rather dull for some time to come. . . ." Today, Levuka's residents value their town as a charming, tranquil relic and treasure the old buildings hurricanes have not swept away.

To help preserve native culture, British officials in Levuka had prohibited further sale of Fijian land to foreigners. They also addressed Fijian labor problems on sugarcane plantations. By custom the native people were used to working for the communal good of village and family, not for the profit of foreign overlords. After forced relocations, many Fijians would run away or attack their masters. To ease a shortage of plantation workers, the first boatload of indentured Indian laborers arrived in 1879.

Through the years, most of the recruits were men. They were of mixed caste, both educated and unschooled; some believed Fiji to be a district near Calcutta. All sought escape, whether from family, religion, poverty, or police, in return for five years of servitude.

India's rigid caste system collapsed quickly in Fiji; despite hardships there was equality—and hope. In 1916, when the last labor ship arrived, more than 60,500 Indians had settled in Fiji. Most chose to stay, and today Indians make up more than half of the population. Many of their traditions endure: music, dance, food, and that enveloping grace, the sari. And their faiths, both Hindu and Muslim, remain strong as well.

"My grandfather came from India on the third boat," young Nitya Nand told me in the Hindu settlement of Korociriciri. "My grandmother, who is now more than ninety, came when she was three years old. They were both from Madras."

Korociriciri is a village of modest houses and riotous flowers scattered across a long ridge overlooking the fertile Rewa Delta; Indian residents lease farmland from Fijian owners. Nitya often stays in Suva, teaching Hindi to American Peace Corps volunteers, but home for him and his family is a house painted bluer than the sky and perched on a windy green hill. A row of palms separates lawn from sheer drop near the edge of the promontory. Dark, jagged mountains pierce the horizon, but below lie miles of flat rice fields. Those nearest were dry and brown with the stubble of last year's harvest. Beyond stretched the irrigated fields of crops half grown.

"Our fields are there." Nitya indicated the richest area of bright green rice and explained that his brothers work the family's eight acres with bullocks and harvest them with machinery leased from the government. "We get three rice crops each year, from eight to ten tons every time, and make about two thousand dollars each harvest." Nitya pointed to the brown, fallow fields. "Those people live outside the irrigation system and have only one crop a year. They must wait for the rains and do everything by hand."

Life moves at a bicycle's pace at the post office and elsewhere in Levuka, Fiji's capital until 1882. Once a brawling port tied to the copra trade, the historic town seeks new prosperity in tourism and tuna-fishing enterprises.

FOLLOWING PAGES: *Realm of living coral dazzles snorkelers in the Yasawas. Formed of lime secretions from polyps, coral reefs fringe most Fijian isles.*

He shook his head sadly. "Even the women must work the fields, and sometimes those families have no harvest at all.

"Come," he said. "I'd like to show you our temple."

We took off our shoes and entered the shrine dedicated to Shiva, a major Hindu god whose immense creative force is believed to maintain the cosmos. Cobras painted on a bright blue wall flanked the entry to the inner chamber where Indian women knelt on Fijian mats to pray, to solicit advice from the attendant, and to lay offerings of fruit and flowers on the black tile altar. The attendant, a soft-spoken matron, presented us with bananas from an offering.

Pictures of Shiva adorned the walls; statues of cobras lined the altar. The serpents wore red hibiscus and marigold blossoms on their heads, and around their thick, hooded necks hung garlands of flowers, strands of beads and shells, and chains with medallions; one wore a crucifix.

"The cobra is Shiva's vehicle," the woman explained. She indicated a bright green snake far larger than the others and a big black lingam, an upright rounded post surrounded by water and representing the god's life-giving energy. "This cobra and lingam have more than doubled in size in

Smartly uniformed in a serrated sulu—*the skirt worn by many native Fijians—a rifle-bearing soldier stands guard outside Government House in Suva, the country's lively capital. A British colony for 96 years, Fiji gained independence in 1970. Above, a craft market and modern shops share a street in Suva, an important cultural and commercial center and, with a population of 70,000, the South Pacific's largest city east of New Zealand.*

Traditions of India pervade Fiji, where Indians make up 53 percent of the population. The transplanted culture thrives in religious celebrations such as Diwali, the Hindu Festival of Lights. At a temple in Suva, worshipers—among them women in saris—proffer food and candles to Lakshmi, Hindu goddess of wealth and prosperity. A minareted mosque (above) further testifies to religious diversity. Indians first came to Fiji in 1879 as indentured laborers to toil in the sugarcane fields. Today they dominate the business and professional life of the country.

the past three weeks," she said matter-of-factly, then added, "In three more days they will double in size again."

Outside, we peeled the bananas and ate them. They had been blessed and were not to be discarded haphazardly.

*I*n Suva, ten days of annual religious ritual, determined by Hindu scripture and the phases of the moon, were drawing to a close. During that time a group of men and boys had lived in seclusion, praying, chanting, resting on mats, and observing a simple diet of fruit and milk—all in preparation for the ceremonies on the final day. I joined the crowd of observers on the lawn of the Holy Mahadevi Mariamman Temple.

John Gopal, a participant for the past six years, later explained the preliminary rituals: "The last night we set fire to huge piles of mangrove logs in a shallow pit about 15 by 30 feet. What an emotional experience to see the beautiful golden color of the wood! For us it has a sacred meaning. We stayed awake all night as the fire burned. People brought food offerings. There were music and prayers to give them peace of heart."

Ceremonies at dawn had taken the participants to the sea. There they immersed themselves in the waters of Suva Harbor—the Fijian substitute for India's sacred Ganges. A priest put them into a trance, pierced their faces, ears, lips, and bodies with sharp metal tridents, and tipped the skewers with marigolds. Attendants and drummers led them six miles through the winding streets of Suva to the temple.

In the pit fronting the temple, the mangrove logs had burned to embers—coals so hot the men who spread them evenly wet their rakes repeatedly to keep the wooden handles from catching fire.

We heard the staccato of drumbeats and then the excited murmur of the crowd as the sacred entourage came into view. They walked barefoot, still dripping from the sea, smeared with ashes. Two balanced massive bouquets of marigolds on their heads. One, wearing a conical hat and draped in gossamer scarlet, clutched a sword edged in red. The other supplicants followed, dressed in yellow cloth tied with scarves the color of flames.

While singers keened sacred songs to the music of strings and drums, the worshipers raced to the pit's edge and one by one walked through, circled to walk again and again, heads thrown back, arms raised in religious ecstasy. Some ground their heels into the embers. Many carried sick children through the pit as a favor to eager parents. The goddess of fire, Draupati, watched from a litter, swathed in colorful fabrics and shaded from the sun's heat by a pink parasol. As a finale the men lifted the litter to their shoulders and circled the pit, then placed the image in the temple.

John, at nonceremonial times an official of the Fiji Visitors Bureau, described the sensations of the ritual: "We are conscious of the heat. We can feel the embers, but they do not burn. During all those days of prayer, the trance, and the journey from the sea on foot, our minds are only on the deity and the fire walk. But as soon as possible after the fire walk we hurry into the temple for the priest to take out the tridents in the presence of the goddess. It must be done while we are still in the trance—at that point we know we may come out of it at any moment. When the priest removes them, we feel no pain, there is no blood. Then it is finished." He smiled. "For the rest of the year the pit is planted in a carpet of marigolds."

Indentured laborers came to Fiji from several parts of India. Those who arrived first usually spoke the village Hindustani of the north; turbaned Sikhs brought the Panjabi language. The majority were southerners who spoke different languages: Tamil, Telugu, Malayalam, or Kannada. To communicate, Indo-Fijians adopted Hindi as their lingua franca.

The old capital of Levuka attracted a few Chinese settlers who established themselves as merchants and importers. Other Chinese immigrants followed—speakers of at least four dialects—and Cantonese became their mutually intelligible tongue.

But native Fijian speakers had the greatest linguistic diversity by far. The country's 14 provinces had hundreds of distinct dialects. It fell to the tiny 20-acre island of Bau, with a dialect of its own, to provide Fiji with a national language. But Fiji's melting pot of peoples needed a cross-cultural lingua franca as well, and so today most people speak English in addition to at least one ancestral tongue.

Westerners in the 19th century found Fiji to be a battle-torn society of rival chiefdoms. Through alliances, wars, and political realignments, the power of the hereditary leaders quickly rose or collapsed. Those divine

Mosaic of cane fields borders the sea on the western side of Viti Levu. Brown patches indicate harvested fields, most of them still cut by cane knife. Grown primarily by Indians, sugarcane remains Fiji's biggest money earner.

FOLLOWING PAGES: *Hospitality Fijian-style calls for a drink of mildly narcotic* yaqona, *or* kava, *ceremoniously prepared by men of Navala village. The ground-up root of a pepper plant, with the flavor of earth and forest,* yaqona *is mixed with water, strained, and then formally drunk from a coconut shell.*

chiefs held absolute sway, killing subjects or roasting captives by unquestioned right or ceremonial whim.

Gradually, chiefs of Bau gained control of a large part of Fiji. When British officials began referring to the Vunivalu, the paramount chief of Bau, as the King of Fiji, he raised no objection and assumed the role with their help. At the same time, Tongans had designs on Fiji. Caught in a morass of political intrigue and debt, the king and other chiefs ceded Fiji to Great Britain in 1874 during the reign of Queen Victoria.

Bau remains a symbol of Fijian history and leadership. "We think of it as sacred," many native Fijians told me. "It's where our old chiefs and the king are buried." Invariably they added wistfully, "And you are going to Bau! I've never been there. Visits are not encouraged."

At low tide Bau can be reached by a causeway across a shallow channel. I arrived there by motorboat with Adi Litia Kaunilotuma Cakobau, the young and vivacious great-great-granddaughter of the king, and with Lily Koroi and Salote Bera of the Fiji Visitors Bureau. For me it was a privileged visit granted few foreigners; for Lily and Salote it was a longtime dream fulfilled; for Adi Kaunilotuma it was a joyous return home.

Lengthening shadows creep into Navala, the last village in Fiji to resist metal roofs and retain only thatched ones on its houses. In outlying villages, hereditary chiefs still arbitrate local disputes and customarily receive gifts from visitors. Recalling a grisly past, Ratu (Chief) Nawawabalavu holds the ax his great-grandfather used to slay a Methodist missionary in 1867. He and his sons pose in grass skirts and boar's tusk amulets.

As we approached the island, we spoke of dialects. Adi Kaunilotuma explained, "There are three ways of speaking our dialect, going back to three different groups here—fishermen, boatbuilders and craftsmen, and . . ."

"The chiefly class," said Lily. "Our national language is an adaptation of that Bauan form. The traditional chiefly form is very difficult. It is a certain way of speaking to the chiefly class. The tone is different; words are totally different. There is a lot of loyalty and respect in it."

On shore, boatbuilders at the south end of the island paused in their work to wave and call greetings to the Adi. "By tradition they live in this area," she said. Long before European contact, Tongans had settled there, bringing their skill of building large oceangoing canoes—a craft that is still honored in Fiji.

Brightly painted houses surrounded by flowers ring the island. Others lie scattered beneath giant trees grown gnarled and dark. A buff-colored hill used as a chiefly necropolis looms above it all. In 1858 missionary Thomas Williams visited Bau and wrote: "The town, bearing the same name as the island, is one of the most striking in appearance of any in Fiji, covering, as it does, a great part of the island with irregularly placed houses of all sizes and tall temples with projecting ridgepoles interspersed with unsightly canoe-sheds."

We strolled across a cricket field in the midst of an open, grassy space. A sea captain's wife, Mary Wallis, described the area's purpose in 1844: "Here they meet to transact public business, to hold *solavus* [rituals for gift giving], to prepare the slaughtered for the ovens, to carve the bodies after they have been cooked, to hold their festive pastimes, &c."

The council house at one end of the plaza has a high-pitched metal roof in the style of ancient thatched temples, and in fact rests on the foundation of an old temple. In the mid-1800s, when the king became a Christian, that shrine to the old ancestral spirits was dismantled and moved across the plaza, and its stones were reassembled into a Wesleyan church. A large white stone against which victims' skulls were crushed in ceremonial sacrifices was moved from the base of the temple steps into the church. It now serves as the baptismal font.

Each Sunday, Ratu (Chief) Sir George Cakobau, the Adi's father and the present Vunivalu of Bau, presides at services along with the minister. Ratu Sir George is the great-grandson of Seru Cakobau, the Fijian king who ceded his homeland to Queen Victoria. In 1970, during the reign of Victoria's great-great-granddaughter Queen Elizabeth II, Fiji regained independence. By happy coincidence, Ratu Sir George was at that time Governor General of Fiji, an office he held until his retirement in 1983.

Lily, Salote, and the Adi sat at the feet of Ratu Sir George in the Cakobau guesthouse, and as prescribed by age-old custom a man of the village joined them to speak ritually in our behalf. We presented a bundle of *yaqona,* or kava, roots to Ratu Sir George in his role as paramount chief of Bau. With ceremony ended, he welcomed us and we chatted.

Ratu Sir George spoke proudly of Fijian sports and international rugby awards. He spoke fondly of his youth, of university days in Australia with his kinsman, the King of Tonga. He spoke expansively of Fiji's modern role in the British Commonwealth and its progressive influence in an emerging South Pacific. "A lot of changes have taken place in the past few years," he said. "The fact that our government is stable and in the hands of capable leaders has enhanced Fiji's image and influence overseas. And our renewed interest in tradition accomplishes what the missionaries intended—the preservation of Fijian culture."

The Adi showed us through the guesthouse, a modern structure of traditional craftsmanship built for the 1982 visit of Queen Elizabeth, with ceilings covered with finely woven mats, beams bound with sennet rope, a canopy bed hung with painted *masi,* or tapa cloth.

"We took a chair outside to the terrace and the Queen sat and enjoyed the breezes," the Adi said. "I think she has a fondness for the sea." My view from the terrace that afternoon was of seabirds in golden light, distant islands, azure channels, and running tide.

A recently paved highway called the Queen's Road runs from Suva down along the south coast of Viti Levu and up its western side. This is Fiji's Coral Coast, known for its great natural beauty and its development in recent years as a tourists' paradise. The road twists along mountain slopes following the rugged shoreline. Each turn of highway, each crest of hill presents vistas of bays, lagoons, offshore islands, and brooding forest. Mangrove thickets edge miles of white sandy beaches.

Occasionally a serene fishing village or an isolated farm punctuates the landscape, but the emphasis is on development—condominiums and large resort hotels promising escape to a tropical Eden. By day visitors swim, sail, or snorkel. Afternoon and evening may bring village entertainment: traditional dances and songs, or demonstrations of a skill that began as a gift from a spirit-god—Fijian fire walking.

It is by eerie coincidence the nation's two largest ethnic groups both perform this awesome feat. For Hindus, fire walking is an annual religious ritual. Fijian fire walkers perform as occasion demands, stepping slowly across hot stones raked clear of burning logs. Tradition says a spirit-god in the form of an eel bestowed the power on the men of Beqa Island in exchange for its life. Today, their kinsmen from other villages also perform.

Quite suddenly, within only a few miles, Viti Levu's flora changes from that of high rainfall to low. Tall grasses swept by sea breezes echo the ripples on turquoise lagoons. I traveled that dry coast in early September—spring in the Southern Hemisphere—and the sugarcane harvest had begun. Cows had been let in to glean fields already cut. They stood facing in every direction with cane stubs bobbling in their mouths like cigars.

Even though it is on the dry side of Viti Levu, the area where the Sigatoka River joins the sea is an unexpected sight on a tropical island. Sahara-like sand dunes flank the river, and dark, wind-exposed hilltops loom like crested waves above them. Prevailing trade winds and water shape and reshape a barren landscape of high, rounded dunes. In contrast, a few miles upriver this lonely wasteland yields to some of Fiji's most fertile farmland: a long, narrow valley nurtured by the river.

For more than a century sugarcane has been Fiji's most profitable industry. But tourism may one day surpass it. It seemed appropriate—a contrast of old and new—that I boarded a cruise ship at the port city of Lautoka, long a sugar-processing center. As Australian, New Zealand, and American tourists set sail in the late afternoon, sugar mills filled the air with smoke that smelled like molasses.

For four days and three nights we cruised the Yasawa Islands, a group scattered to the northwest of Viti Levu and edging a peaceful sea some call the Blue Lagoon. Tradition named it Bligh Water, for it was through these tranquil waters that Capt. William Bligh and members of his crew passed on their journey of desperation after the *Bounty* mutineers put them into an open boat. Bligh recorded that on the morning of May 7, 1789, "we now observed two large sailing canoes coming swiftly after us along shore, and, being apprehensive of their intentions, we rowed with some anxiety, being sensible of our weak and defenseless state. . . . Only one of the canoes gained upon us, and by three o'clock in the afternoon was not more than two miles off, when she gave over chase."

But ours were days of pampered peace. Passengers relaxed on board, cavorted in the sea, and visited islands. We climbed into a cave to plunge into a brilliant blue pool below. We snorkeled, suspended above undersea forests of bright coral and plants where tropical fish browsed and usually furtive sea snakes stretched out in branching shade.

Our Fijian crew praised the local village life-style. Sili, married to a Yasawan woman, told me, "Life in a village is the best of all—no tax, no electricity bill, no water bill. If you want to build a house, just start it. Help will automatically come. Everyone in a village is related, and each village is just like a company; the chief is the director and looks after everything."

One evening at an island stop, Chief Tevita—known as Chief David—

Preparations for fire walking proceed as Fijians in grass skirts and garlands rake a bed of stones heated for hours under blazing logs. Believing their skill to come from a god, the men will walk barefoot—and unscathed—over the scorching stones. Fijian customs, especially cannibalism, shocked early European visitors. In a land where people once praised food as tasting as "tender as a dead man," a carved cannibal fork (above) now serves only the appetite of souvenir hunters.

and performers from his village nearby joined us on a torchlit beach. Women in long dresses with tapa-cloth designs danced, sang, and flourished palm fans to the rhythm of drums and bamboo instruments. Bare-chested men in grass skirts sang, swayed, leaped, and twirled.

One brandished a spear close to my face and scowled ominously as he danced, then broke into a grin and offered to teach me "the Fijian version of do-si-do." He was Chief David's son, the future chief, and as we put an arm around each other's waist and shuffled hip-to-hip through the sand he begged forgiveness for dancing slowly: "A rugby injury to my knee. I played on the championship Nadi team." The young men repeatedly asked a pretty Australian teenager named Renae to dance. The women hung garlands of sweetly perfumed frangipani around each tourist's neck.

The next afternoon I stood at the ship's stern with Renae as we returned to Lautoka. We still wore the flowers, now wilting but no less fragrant. "I was told if you throw them into the sea you will return," she said.

We leaned over the railing and dropped our garlands into the Blue Lagoon. They floated across the foaming wake. Then, carried into the current and swept by the tide, they drifted toward a small, uninhabited island with palm trees and a spot of beach. The island could not have been more than an acre or two—just large enough for a fantasy of paradise.

We did not talk again or turn away until it faded from view.

Beachcombing the leisurely way brings tourists to a shell market in the Yasawa Islands. Warm, crystalline waters nearby entice a snorkeler. Their numbers growing, vacationers in Fiji often follow the advice given by many islanders: Live for today, tomorrow is tomorrow.

PRECEDING PAGES: *Sunset extravaganza over Mana Island marks the end of another* siga totoka—*fine day—in the South Seas.*

FRENCH POLYNESIA

Isles of Tahiti

By Christine Eckstrom Lee
Photographs by Nicholas DeVore III

A white flower blooms on the summit of Mount Temehani on the is-land of Raiatea. Its name, *tiare apetahi,* means "one-sided flower," and its five petals are like the fingers of a hand, reaching up. Each morning new buds open just before dawn with a pop that can be heard. In one legend, the flower is the hand of an island princess who said as she died in her lov-er's arms, "Every morning when you come to the mountain, I will give you my hand to caress."

Long ago, the flower, the mountain, and the island were held sacred by the Polynesian people who sailed from Tonga and Samoa toward the ris-ing sun to discover the vast constellation of islands sprinkled across the heart of the South Pacific. Over time, Raiatea became the religious, cultur-al, and political center of the newly settled isles. The people called it Havai'i—the homeland—perhaps in remembrance of Savai'i, a Samoan is-land they left behind. They believed that when they died their spirits soared to Havai'i, to the top of Temehani, where they entered *Rohutu-no'ano'a,* the fragrant paradise. The flower that bloomed there was forbid-den, taboo, and as if in proof of its special nature it remains a botanical mystery: The tiare apetahi cannot be transplanted. It will grow nowhere else in the world except on the high slopes of Temehani.

Unique, beautiful, the tiare apetahi is a living symbol of the islands known as French Polynesia. They lie in the trade-wind tropics south of the Equator, about midway between Australia and South America. Scattered across an ocean region about half the size of the contiguous United States, the 130-odd islands of French Polynesia have a total land area only slightly larger than Rhode Island. France made the islands a protectorate in the 1840s, and they are now a French overseas territory, with its center of

Fragile emblem of paradise, a tiare apetahi—*one-sided flower—blooms on Raiatea's Mount Temehani, the only known place on earth the plant grows.* PRECEDING PAGES: *Tropical sunlight illumines the mirrorlike Baie de Maroe at Huahine. Since the time of European discovery, writers, artists, and adventurers have celebrated the grandeur of French Polynesia.*

FLOWER ART: TIARE TAHITI *(Gardenia taitensis);* PHOTOGRAPH BY DAVID HISER

government on Tahiti, the largest and most populous isle. Often referred to collectively as Tahiti, the islands consist of five archipelagoes: the low coral atolls of the Tuamotus and the high volcanic isles of the Marquesas, the Australs, the Gambiers, and the Societies—the last of which include Tahiti and Raiatea.

D̲ark clouds enveloped the peaks of Temehani the morning I climbed the mountain. Three island boys who knew the route to the summit—2,500 feet up—led me there with my friend and interpreter Tiare Sanford and photographer David Hiser. The trail to the top is precipitous and overgrown; our guides carried machetes. We threaded our way through groves of banana trees and palms, Tahitian chestnuts and pandanus, and through thickets of dripping ferns that reached above our heads. We crossed small streams and inched up slippery rock walls. Part of the time, we crawled. High in the forest we heard the melancholy cry of the 'u'upa, a green bird said to be the shadow of the ghosts that haunt the woods.

Halfway up, we stopped to drink from a stream. As I knelt and cupped my hands in the water, a blossom floated by, pure white against the dark streambed, as startling as a snowflake. It was a tiare apetahi, and it came like a gift from the mountain.

The summit plateau was an up-and-down place of rocky peaks and slopes. It rained, and clouds swept by below us. We scanned the hills. Across a deep valley, just above a stream, we spotted a bush with three white blossoms. Against the gray sky and dark greenery, they seemed as bright as magnolias in Mississippi. Up close, the shrub was unremarkable; the flowers were like porcelain. Tiare and I broke off branches and stuck them in the soil to propagate new plants, and we picked the blossoms and wore them in our hair, Polynesian style.

"This is the real Tahiti," said Tiare. "This is the beauty of my land." A young woman of Tahitian and French descent, Tiare was educated in Europe and the United States and has traveled around the world, but she returned to Tahiti to live. "If I am away from Tahiti for too long, I begin to fade like a flower," she said.

Far below, the lagoon of Raiatea encircled the island, a pool of liquid turquoise rimmed by a barrier reef. Breakers crashed on the coral, rolling down the reef in a horizontal white line. To the east rose the island of Huahine, its green heights wreathed in clouds. Bora Bora, where Tiare was born, floated on the northwestern horizon like a mountainous blue mirage. Legend says that Raiatea gave birth to these and other islands to the sound of the drumbeat of the sea.

"Tahiti is peace," said Tiare. "There is a serenity of life here that you will not find anywhere else in the world." She sang songs of Bora Bora and Temehani as we descended the mountain. "If you are lucky enough to have a Tahitian mother, you will learn the old songs and legends," she said. "They will tell you the story of Tahiti."

Long before the first European ships appeared on the horizon, Polynesian priests and seers had predicted their arrival. In the late 18th century, the explorers came to the island of Tahiti: the Englishman Samuel Wallis in 1767; the Frenchman Louis Antoine de Bougainville in 1768; and Capt. James Cook, on the first of his three voyages, in 1769. All were amazed by what they found. Tahiti was called the Queen of the Pacific, the Garden of Eden, where the men were handsome and strong, the women stately and beautiful. Their pleasurable life-style, in easy harmony with a luxuriant natural world and enriched by a love of land and sea, was described by some as superior to that of Western man.

Tahitians fished from outrigger canoes and dived for pearls in the atoll lagoons. Men knew the sea and the stars. Women wove fine mats and decorative objects from pandanus and palm fronds. People raised taro and yams and picked ripe bananas, breadfruit, and coconuts from trees that grew by their homes. Everywhere, every day, a blend of religion, romance, and mysticism pervaded life in Tahiti.

All was not idyllic. There were wars and human sacrifice and, especially on larger islands such as Tahiti and Raiatea, a highly stratified society ruled by chiefs and priests. Warfare soon ended and the social structure changed with the arrival of the Europeans, but the past was not forgotten.

Tahiti had no written language when Cook arrived. The history of the people was oral, memorized and repeated from island to island. The stories of the creation of the world and the deeds of the gods and heroes, of the ancestors and their great oceanic voyages, of the lands that lay beyond the horizon—the Polynesian past was preserved in epic poetry set to rhythmic chant. Often the legends were told in dance to the beat of drums. Today, many Tahitians can still recite their ancient lineage, and the descendants of former royal families are known and remembered.

French Polynesia embraces some 130 volcanic and coral islands spanning an ocean area of more than 1.5 million square miles—about the size of Western Europe. Some 160,000 people live in this French overseas territory.

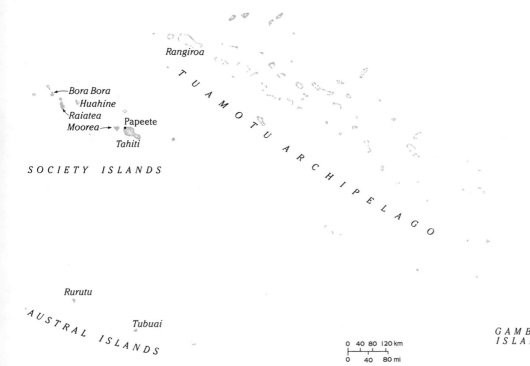

Foreign perceptions of Tahiti may have changed little since the days of discovery, but in fact life on Tahiti has changed with the times, with the arrival of each ship, each plane, each new thing from the outside world. Tapa yielded to cotton; metal replaced stone. Missionaries brought Christianity and destroyed old religious sites. After annexation, Tahitians learned French and children read about Napoleon in school. Trading ships brought manufactured goods that replaced handcrafted ones. Coconut- and pandanus-thatched roofs gave way to tin. Cars and motor scooters appeared; roads were paved; and in 1960 airplanes first landed on Tahiti. In the mid-sixties, France began nuclear testing on remote atolls in the Tuamotus; money and military personnel poured in, bolstering Tahiti's economy. The controversial testing, now underground, continues.

Elements of the old culture still live, some as a revival of the past and some as an integral part of life that has never changed. Each year, Tahiti celebrates its folklore and traditions in a festival called Tiurai—the Tahitian word for July—a time when people from islands as far away as Hawaii and Samoa come to Tahiti for parades, exhibitions, and sporting events that proclaim the exuberant heritage of Polynesia.

I arrived in Tahiti in the middle of Tiurai. The waterfront in Papeete, the capital and chief port of French Polynesia, was lined with bright-colored

Sacred stones of a centuries-old marae—*an open-air temple platform—edge the shore on Raiatea, the island cherished as the spiritual homeland of eastern Polynesia and a dispersal point for ancient voyages of discovery.*

FOLLOWING PAGES: *Yachts from around the world line the waterfront of Papeete, capital and economic hub of French Polynesia, on the volcanic isle of Tahiti.*

94

outrigger racing canoes and crowded with spectators and paddlers wearing fresh flower crowns and wild-patterned *pareu*—lengths of cloth creatively wrapped and tied. Moored at the water's edge were yachts from around the world. Scores of canoes filled the glassy harbor, practicing for various races. The sleek voyaging canoes that once ranged across the lonely Pacific were the glory of Polynesia, and canoe races are the most popular events of Tiurai. Hundreds of Tahitians jammed the shores, laughing, picnicking, and making bets. Vendors sold food and sweet leis of *tiare Tahiti,* the native gardenia that scents the isles. Next to me were two older women, round as rolls, wearing long, red-and-white floral dresses and blossoms tucked behind their ears. They sat like dolls in the warm sun, legs outstretched, gossiping and giggling and wiggling their toes.

Women as well as men raced, and in the one-woman race, two paddlers approached the finish line in a dead heat. People began to cheer more loudly than ever and pointed at one of the racers. She was just behind the leader, and in her furious paddling she had lost her top. Undaunted, she paddled harder—and won the race, to a round of applause and whistles.

From a boat in the harbor, I watched some of the races and stared up at the towering beauty of Tahiti. Above the red-roofed buildings of Papeete, bright green mountains reach more than a mile into the sky, their steep slopes rough and shadowy with ravines and hills.

More than half of French Polynesia's 160,000 people live on Tahiti, and half of Tahiti lives in or near Papeete. During Tiurai, the city that is the hub of modern French Polynesia is transformed into a showcase for its old culture. A week-long singing and dancing competition held under the stars drew thousands of people, and each day at the park called Place Tarahoi, artisans and others demonstrated their skills: carving, weaving, Polynesian quilting, the making of flower and shell crowns and leis, and the preparation of *po'e* and other foods. Crowds joined in as groups of men and women sang old songs, danced, and told stories and legends.

Ironically, Tiurai began more than a century ago as a parade to celebrate Bastille Day, the French national holiday on July 14. In grand Tahitian style, the festivities grew from a day to a month, but the July 14 parade in Papeete is still a centerpiece of Tiurai—and a tangible display of the blend of France and Polynesia that shapes life in modern Tahiti.

I stood among the masses of people flanking the Avenue Général de Gaulle to watch the parade. Some 800 French military men and women marched by to the slow beat of drums and the music of patriotic songs. There were cheers for the women, the sailors, and the foreign legionnaires. Beside me, a beautiful young Tahitian woman waved to a soldier; her little daughter, arms around her mother's neck, kissed her on the face and shoulder, ignoring the parade.

Around a corner, a block-long train of Tahitian floats waited to follow the armed forces. Drummers and other musicians warmed up, imitating the military drumrolls and then breaking into fast Polynesian rhythms. The people watching the solemn military parade shook their hips to the beat from around the corner and clapped and cheered wildly when the Tahitian floats appeared, decked with flowers, joyous with song. Each had a theme: traditional crafts, Tahitian revelry, the feelings of those from smaller islands who come to live in Tahiti, and the initiation of a Frenchwoman into the island way of life by a group of lovely *vahine*—women of Tahiti. The

military parade was brief, but an hour after it had ended, the Tahitian floats were still in the street, surrounded by people singing and dancing.

Beyond Papeete, with its French foods and wines and fashions, its Renaults and Peugeots, Tahiti is quiet and rural. I drove the road that circles the island, passing women selling fresh fish and fruit at roadside stands and young girls with long, dark hair, strolling barefoot, dressed in pretty pareu. High hedgerows of red, yellow, and green crotons and scarlet hibiscus edged tidy yards full of strutting chickens and sleeping dogs. The land was musical with swaying palms. All colors were bright and pure: blue sea, white waves, green land. Ripe yellow papayas shone amid dark green leaves; sprays of pink bougainvillea arched into a cobalt sky. From a lane that wound into a valley, I walked a path to a lush spot where rushing water tumbled from a cliff a few hundred feet high. Looking up at a cathedral of mountain peaks, I stood under the showering falls and swam in a clear pool, washed of all thoughts of a world beyond Tahiti.

*T*he colors and mood of the countryside recall the paintings of Paul Gauguin, the French artist who lived in Tahiti in the late 19th century. His work immortalized the grandeur of the land, the simplicity of "life in the open," the melancholy beauty of the Polynesian women, the innate mystery of Tahiti. "All the joys—animal and human—of a free life are mine," he wrote. "I have escaped everything that is artificial, conventional, customary. I am entering into the truth, into nature." He lived like a native in a bamboo-and-pandanus *fare,* or house, wearing a pareu and enjoying the company of a young vahine. But he was plagued by poor health, financial troubles, and a tortured mind. He died in 1903 in the Marquesas—where he had gone in search of a place even more unspoiled than Tahiti.

Gauguin was a wave in the stream of artists and writers who have journeyed to Tahiti: Herman Melville, Robert Louis Stevenson, Rupert Brooke, Somerset Maugham, Zane Grey, Henri Matisse, James Michener. The lure of French Polynesia has not diminished, although many artists now live on the island of Moorea, 12 miles west of Tahiti across the Sea of the Moon.

At dusk, the eyes of Papeete turn to Moorea, haloed in sunset colors, looking like a distant reflection of Tahiti. Moorea changes every day, sometimes wrapped in a colorful pareu of clouds, sometimes naked against the blue dome of the sky.

To reach the island, I took the *Tamarii Moorea,* a big ferry loaded with cement, cinder blocks, wire, tires, flour, beer, and passengers. One traveler played a guitar, and during the hour-long trip he led the others in song. At the small dock in Vai'are, on Moorea's east coast, the supplies were unloaded and crates of pineapples, bananas, and taro were stacked aboard, bound for Tahiti.

From the sea, Moorea presents a dramatic emerald-in-the-rough profile of peaks. The mountains rise sharply from the shore; each stands alone, fashioned into strange forms by weathering. Above the bay of Vai'are,

Skirts of shredded hibiscus bark swish to the beat of drums as Rurutu islanders perform at a hotel in Papeete. Once banned by disapproving missionaries, dancing has seen a spirited revival, and preserves for Polynesians the cultural traditions and legends of their ancestors.

palms climb the walls of hills, and the noonday sun shimmers on the waving fronds like phosphorescence.

In Cook's Bay, one of two deep cuts in the coastline that give Moorea the shape of a three-lobed heart, I stopped to visit with Dutch artist Aad van der Heyde at his gallery-studio-shop by the sea. Aad first saw Tahiti in 1956, on his way to Australia. He returned a few years later with a suitcase of paints and brushes and built a fare in Mataiea on Tahiti. He learned to live like a Tahitian—"simply, like a beachcomber"—and later discovered that his fare was a few hundred yards from where Gauguin had lived. In 1964 he settled on Moorea, where he has stayed ever since with his lovely Tahitian wife, Augustine. When I met him, he was dressed in a brown-and-white pareu and surrounded by the paintings of local artists and display cases of Pacific arts and crafts.

"I am a romantic," he told me. "There is real romance living here on Moorea. And there is still real adventure in the South Pacific."

Aad is 50, and he looks as young as he does in his old photographs. He showed me a picture of himself on the beach with his easel; his fishing nets were draped in the trees. "I enjoy catching my own fish, sleeping in my canoe next to my nets, and seeing the stars reflected in the lagoon," he said. "You look up, there are stars; you look down, there are stars; and you know that beyond the stars there's your net and your food.

"This life is very free, very basic. The natural environment is generous— the lagoon, the reef, the fertile valleys—people can afford to be hospitable, and a little carefree. I have *time* for things. Time to read, time for music, time to repair a canoe or a net, to hike in the mountains, to sail, to paint. What would my life have been outside Tahiti? I don't even ask any more."

We walked through his outdoor gallery in a garden. I admired his work—portraits and landscapes painted with heavy strokes, dark and mysterious, the timeless Tahiti.

"When I first came here," Aad told me, "inevitably the expatriates would say, 'Ah, but you should have been here 20 years ago. Tahiti has changed.' Captain Cook on his second voyage said that Tahiti wasn't what it used to be. But there is still a strong traditional life here—and a very long social ladder. You have the simple fisherman with his spear and his net and his canoe, and you have the man who hops into his private plane and flies to Tahiti. The people in Papeete go to the outer islands to get back in touch with nature, and the people on the outer islands are dreaming of a Mercedes Benz and a video machine."

He showed me his house, full of primitive art of the South Pacific and pretty quilts handmade by Augustine. "Yesterday I took Augustine to her adopted mother," he said. "She lives deep in a valley, an idyllic place. Beautiful mountains all around, horses tied up in the front yard. They heat their water in big black pots over a wood fire. On the way there we passed a lawyer from Tahiti on his horse. In Tahiti he drives a Mercedes, plays tennis, lives the fast life. Here he is in Moorea, riding his horse early in the morning. Many Tahitians still get away with living in both worlds.

"Here you don't really need much to live if you have your land. I am like a Tahitian; I have everything I want—a beautiful wife and daughter, some land, my home, this life. This is my security—and my adventure."

One hundred and fifty miles northwest of Tahiti lies an island as lovely as its evocative name: Bora Bora. It is an island castle, its moat a turquoise lagoon encircled by a barrier reef and *motu*—coral islets, thick with palms, that have grown up from the reef. In the midday sun, the colors of the lagoon are so intense that snow-white terns flying above it appear blue. The island is crowned by 2,400-foot Mount Otemanu, a rock peak that looks, from different angles, like a giant adz head, a high-backed throne, or the blade of a sword.

Like the other high isles of French Polynesia, Bora Bora is slowly becoming an atoll. The volcanic fires that propelled the island up from the ocean floor died long ago, and Bora Bora is imperceptibly sinking into the sea from which it arose. As the island subsides, the surrounding reef grows higher; ages from now, a low coral ring around an empty lagoon will mark the site where an island went down.

I circled the island in a small boat with Erwin Christian, a German photographer and diver who has lived there for many years. "Bora Bora has the best of both Polynesian worlds—the high mountains like Tahiti and a beautiful lagoon like the atolls," he explained. "But because of its beauty,

Tahiti's crown, Orohena, rises more than a mile into the sky—higher than the clouds drifting across an interior veined with waterfalls. Volcanoes thrust Tahiti up from the ocean floor; wind and rain sculptured the land.

FOLLOWING PAGES: *Faces of Tahiti reflect a blend of nationalities. The serene grace and beauty of island women, legendary since the days of Captain Cook, were immortalized in the paintings of French artist Paul Gauguin.*

Bora Bora has succumbed to tourism more than any other island. These people used to be kings in their own land. Little by little they are offering up pieces of their culture, sacrifices to tourism. There must be a better balance, or the culture that visitors come to see will be lost."

The problem is complex, and it concerns all inhabitants of French Polynesia. Evidence of cultural erosion is hard to see; the islands look the same, but when I drove the circle road around Bora Bora, I noticed few taro patches and vegetable gardens, and few fishermen in the lagoon. I stopped to talk with a young girl preparing pandanus for thatching roofs. Her own house had a tin roof; the pandanus, she explained, was for the roofs of tourist bungalows.

In his show at the Hotel Marara, a Tahitian performer named Simplet describes with gentle humor the changes that have come to Bora Bora and the realities of island living. To have the material goods that make life easier, he explains, Tahitians must change their traditional ways. If they work all day at a tourist hotel, they don't have time to plant taro and go fishing and make pandanus roofs for their homes. They must buy imported food and tin roofs—and earn more money, so that finally, when they retire, they can relax and live like real Tahitians.

DAVID HISER

Emerald peaks and translucent waters of Moorea, Tahiti's sister isle, offer an unspoiled retreat from the bustle of Papeete for vacationers and artists alike. Lacy breakers on the barrier reef trace a turquoise lagoon rich in fish and colorful corals. Twelve miles away, Tahiti commands the eastern horizon.

Simplet took a break from helping his son build a fishing boat to speak with me one afternoon. "We have big troubles now," he said. "Many young ones don't want to learn their own way of life. I say to them, Tahitians are very lucky in the world. We are very popular. But soon we will be like an empty bottle—nice outside, nothing inside. I tell the young, it's easy to live if you will learn. And you must learn, because someday there will be no more money."

Visitors at the Hotel Marara stay in traditional thatch-roofed fare by the sea, built by Dino de Laurentiis in 1977 to house the crew making the film *Hurricane*. Simplet pointed to a row of outrigger canoes on the beach. They were built for the movie. "Lucky for us the movie people came," he said, "because they showed us how the canoes were made 200 years ago. I say to the young, one day the European will come to Tahiti and show you how to prepare Tahitian food.

"All my life, I'm happy," he continued. "I fish, I go to the mountains for oranges and wild bananas—early in the morning when the air is oh, so fresh. With a coconut tree and bamboo, I can build my house. Easy! I tell the young, the work is fun if you do it with your heart." Sitting by the sea, he sang a song, soft and low, "Bora Bora ē! I cry because I love my country, Bora Bora ē!"

The Americans came to Bora Bora in World War II. There they built the first airstrip in French Polynesia, and more than 5,000 soldiers were stationed on the island James Michener immortalized as Bali-ha'i in his *Tales of the South Pacific*. The Americans left a lasting impression on Bora Bora, which has a population of only 3,200.

In the main village of Vaitape, I saw something I had seen nowhere else in Polynesia: a hamburger stand. An incongruous mix of things Tahitian, French, and American, Bora Bora Burgers is open-air, with tree-trunk stools, a wooden counter covered with fresh red hibiscus blossoms, four bubble-gum machines, and an espresso coffee maker. People stop by for Cokes and snacks and to visit with the owner, Marguerite, who wears a splashy pareu. A Frenchman sat down next to me and exchanged gossip with Marguerite in French. Ordering a hot dog, he said, "Ah, Marguerite, if only I could have some red wine with it!" A young Tahitian woman, barefoot and wearing a pareu, walked up and spoke with Marguerite in Tahitian. Marguerite pulled a cage of French fries out of hot oil; burgers sizzled on the grill. *"Hina'aro vau e 'amu ī te* hamburger," said the young woman, placing her order. She shifted to French. *"Et un* Sprite, *eh?"* "OK," said Marguerite. "No problem."

South of Vaitape, facing the setting sun, is a small restaurant-bungalow complex called Bloody Mary's, after the character in *Tales of the South Pacific*. The owner, Baron George Von Dangel, is a tall man of commanding presence. He has been called a pretender to the throne of Poland, a direct descendant of Alexander the Great, an exorcist and healer. He is a physician, he told me, and a former fighter pilot in the Australian Air Force, and he has had roles in Hollywood films. Indisputably he is a gregarious host, an excellent cook, and a wonderful raconteur.

"It is still Michener here—it's 'Rascals in Paradise,' " he said as we sat on palm-trunk stools in his thatch-roofed, sand-floored restaurant. Fresh fish smoked on a barbecue grill and sweet Polynesian music played. He told stories of celebrities stopping in at Bloody Mary's, of visits by Dorothy

"Polynesia has always attracted dreamers," says Dutch artist Aad van der Heyde, who has lived on Moorea since 1964. In verdant settings like those that inspired Gauguin, Aad finds subjects for his portraits and landscapes. His daughter Nane, at left, and model Laina Grell accompany him to a location on Moorea where he will continue work on a painting. In 1975 French Polynesia chose Aad's portrait of a Tahitian vahine *(above) for use on a postage stamp, now a collector's item.*

Lamour, Julio Iglesias, and Sheikh Yamani; of one evening when Jimmy Buffett played songs all night and another when Dudley Moore tended bar and delighted the sudsy regulars, who told him he should be an actor.

The baron spoke of expatriates and eccentrics drawn to a life in the islands. "Why do these misfits come here?" he asked. "Those with an extroverted sense of life? The truth is here, the beauty is here, the magic is here. If you try to leave, the islands pull you back. Polynesians are so unaffected, so unspoiled. They feel people through their eyes. They see your soul."

His wife, Pauline, is a beautiful young woman with wide, dark eyes. "Pauline is of the royal family of Rimatara, in the Austral Islands," the baron averred. "She has her mother's gift of seeing."

Pauline told me of the strange things that are said to occur when someone important dies. "When my grandmother was dying, the island became dark and the sea was agitated. All was black. When the storm finished, she was gone. This happened because she was the queen."

The baron told me legends of Polynesia—the origin of the coconut tree, why there is daylight, and the story of the goddess Pele, Queen of the Volcano, who was born in the once-fiery mountain on Bora Bora and left to live in Hawaii. "We don't know if she'll ever come back," he said.

We all walked outside to look at the stars. The Milky Way was a winking cloud in a black sky luminous with southern constellations, and Jupiter and Mars gleamed pink. "I love to be here on full-moon nights when the stardust is on the water," the baron said. "But tonight on Bora Bora we can see the universe."

*I*f the ancient canoes had left paths in the sea, the Polynesian Pacific would be crosshatched with trails. Even Captain Cook was stunned by the navigational feats implied by the settlement of islands thousands of miles apart by one people. At the time of Cook's arrival, the Tahitians still knew the locations of faraway isles where the ancestors had settled, but they had stopped roaming the high seas, and legends preserved their history.

Tracing the origins of the Polynesians, the sequence of island settlement, and the evolution of island societies has been a difficult task for archaeologists. They are faced with a people who had a strong oral tradition but a largely perishable material culture. Piece by piece, the puzzle of the Polynesian past is being assembled, and one of the great puzzle masters is Dr. Yosihiko H. Sinoto, chairman of the Department of Anthropology at the Bernice P. Bishop Museum in Honolulu. At a site on Huahine, a hundred miles northwest of Tahiti, Dr. Sinoto found a jumble of jigsaw pieces.

Luck and the growth of tourism played a role in the discovery of the site near the main village of Fare on Huahine's west coast. In 1972, workers were dredging a swampy area by the sea to create a landscape of ponds and high ground for the new Hotel Bali Hai. As they dug down, artifacts

Still life on Moorea: Pauline Teariki sits in Sunday repose outside the guesthouse she owns and manages in the town of Afareaitu; an islander carries produce to market—an activity depicted in the paintings of Gauguin.

FOLLOWING PAGES: *Last light breaks through clouds veiling the jagged peaks of Moorea as an outrigger canoe skims across calm waters west of Tahiti.*

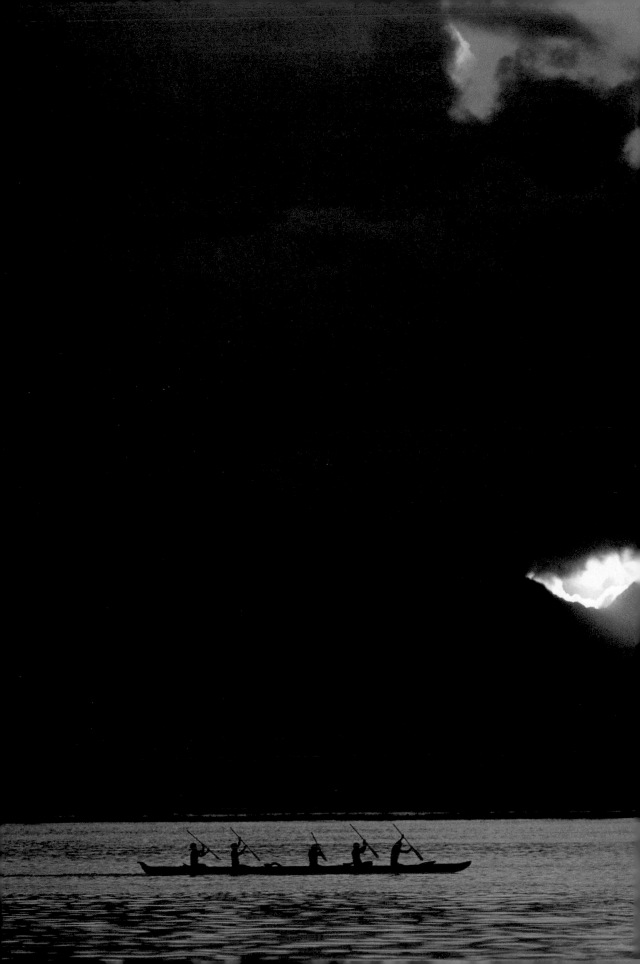

came up, among them a whalebone *patu*—a hand weapon until then believed unique to the Maori warriors of New Zealand.

At the time, Dr. Sinoto was in the village of Maeva on Huahine, reconstructing stone *marae*—ancient religious platforms. Workers told him about the patu, and he rushed to the construction site. With the cooperation of the Hotel Bali Hai, Dr. Sinoto has been excavating there ever since, uncovering a village that dates back to A.D. 850—the oldest known one in the Society Islands and among the most remarkable finds in all of Polynesia. His discoveries on Huahine lend support to the theory that the Polynesians migrated east from Tonga and Samoa around A.D. 300, arriving first in the Marquesas and then traveling south to the Societies. From there they later voyaged to Hawaii and New Zealand, the northern and southern points of the Polynesian triangle that reaches east to Easter Island.

Dr. Sinoto showed me around the site, set in a palm grove behind some hotel bungalows. Pumps drew water from soggy digging pits, and teams of workers at tables washed mounds of mud, sifting for artifacts. It was hot, and mosquitoes swarmed.

"I prospected this area in 1963, walking along the beach," said Dr. Sinoto. "I thought, who could live in a place like this? So I passed it by. After the patu was discovered and I began excavating here, I realized what had happened. Sometime around A.D. 1000, a tidal wave hit this place and all activity suddenly stopped. The village was covered with white beach sand, and the people left. The site is still waterlogged, and artifacts that normally decay in air are preserved in water underground, scattered just as the tidal wave left them. We are finding everyday objects in all stages of production. Some people have called this the Polynesian Pompeii."

Elaine Jourdane, one of Dr. Sinoto's assistants, walked up with a pearl-shell fishhook in her hand. "The first time! What a beauty!" said Dr. Sinoto. "This is a hook point for a bonito fishing lure—we've never found one here before. You find it in New Zealand, Hawaii, Tonga, Samoa, the Marquesas, and now we have it here."

Fishhooks are one of Dr. Sinoto's specialties. He has even made his own and tested their efficiency in the lagoons of the Tuamotus. "Fishhooks and adz heads and other artifacts help us establish a cultural assemblage," he explained. "I had a good idea from my work in the Marquesas what sorts of things I might find here." In the 1960s Dr. Sinoto found a site in the Marquesas that is the oldest known settlement in eastern Polynesia, dating to A.D. 300. "When I began here, I told my workers, 'If you find this type of fishhook or this adz head, I'll buy you a drink.' That was my mistake, because I had to take them to the bar every day!"

In 1977 Dr. Sinoto made his most startling discovery: parts of an ancient voyaging canoe—the oldest in Polynesia. "The canoe was not finished," Dr. Sinoto explained. "That's what makes it so interesting. When Cook came to Tahiti, he saw big double canoes in the harbor, and he asked the people who built such canoes. They said Raiatea and Huahine islanders. They carried on the tradition, and here is a canoe. I'm still looking for more parts." He showed me a ten-foot-long piece of wood in a pit of water; it was probably part of the canoe's bow, just unearthed.

"Before I worked this site, I suspected a Marquesas-Tahiti-New Zealand connection. The whalebone patu and other artifacts—such as adz and harpoon heads—helped establish the material link between the Society

Islands and New Zealand. The Maori ancestors probably left for New Zealand from the Societies, as the legends say. We have the evidence—now we have a canoe."

We walked to the beach, where some of his team were taking a break, swimming. "The old people of Huahine say the shoreline has come in over the past 50 years," he said. "Part of this site is out there, in the sea." He glanced near my feet. "What is that?" He reached down and picked up a worked shell. "Look—this is a coconut scraper. Everywhere you go, you find things. And now Tahitians bring me things *they* find. When I first started working on Huahine, rebuilding the marae at Maeva, I had a hard time getting workers. Tahitians don't want to touch the ancient stones. They believe the stones still have power, and some are afraid. But when they saw me working, they started wondering, 'How did the ancestors do it?' I began to get volunteers, and now they are proud."

Dr. Sinoto's involvement with Tahitian society extends beyond the past. "I rebuilt an old meetinghouse at Maeva as part of a project sponsored by the Tahiti Tourist Board," he said. "Local people came inside and said, 'My goodness, how cool this is.' I said, 'This is your traditional house. This is the one your ancestors built.' So now some young couples are building houses like that."

The pioneering work of Dr. Sinoto and others has sparked new interest in Polynesian society—past and present—but many questions remain unanswered. "People ask me, 'Why did the Polynesians go to sea? Why did they leave for new lands when they didn't have to go?' There is no easy explanation," said Dr. Sinoto. "I have what I call my romantic theory. Polynesians are a seafaring people. For them, the ocean is a garden. They see the birds migrating from distant lands, and they know the lands are there. They have navigational skills. So they get in their oceangoing canoes with their families and their food, and they follow the birds."

Several hundred miles south of Tahiti lies a group of isles called the Australs, treasured by culture-conscious Tahitians as a keeper of island traditions and the old way of life. Few tourists visit the remote Australs, but in recent years small airports have opened on the two main islands, Rurutu and Tubuai. Like the trading ships of old, airplanes now bring change—rapid communication, visitors, the accoutrements of modern life. The plane to Rurutu was packed with islanders heading home, wearing sweet-scented farewell leis and carrying big boxes of presents and goods. At the back of the plane, puppies whined and hens clucked.

In the village of Moerai on Rurutu, I walked along the sandy main street, past well-kept homes and yards with flowers, fruit trees, and lush vegetable gardens. Curtains of pandanus were draped over trees to dry, and fat pigs were tethered to the trunks. Two young boys passed by on horseback, and in the late afternoon people walked to a meeting at the Protestant church, the heart of the village.

On Sunday morning I went to church. I sat in a plain wood pew awash in soft sunlight pouring in from open windows, and listened to the congregation sing the rich, hypnotic choral hymns known in French Polynesia as *hīmene*. Missionaries taught the Polynesians Protestant hymns, and the people adapted them to their own singing traditions, producing a new and beautiful style of music. All singing was a cappella, and everyone sang. A silence would be broken by the high wail of an older mama, launching the people into song. The men would join in, chanting a deep bass line, and groups of women would harmonize the melody lines, overlaid with the high descants of the older mamas. All singers returned to a single tone at the end, and I understood why some of the old hīmene have been compared to intricate lacework.

After church I visited Ingrid Drollet, a Tahitian who works as a teacher on the island. "Curiously, Rurutu is both a stronghold of the Protestant church and a place where Polynesian traditions are preserved," she said. "The church provides a firm social structure, and within that structure community life is strong. Communal work—*pupu*—is still the backbone of society here. The people of Rurutu don't know how to live individually. This makes them very strong."

The next day, Ingrid took photographer Nicholas DeVore and me to the pretty village of Avera, to visit a women's weaving group. Rurutu is famous for its fine mats, baskets, and hats made of pandanus, bamboo, and coconut, and the women of Avera are among the island's best weavers. We met them in the small thatched house where they work and display their crafts. They sat in a circle on a huge pandanus mat, preparing fibers, weaving, and talking; each wore a bright Sunday dress and a fresh crown of blossoms. After a while, they began to sing softly, "Hina! Hina!"

"They are singing the song of Hina," Ingrid told me. "The legends say she was the last cannibal woman of Rurutu. She lived alone in a cave, high in a mountain in the middle of the island. One day some fishermen saw smoke coming from her cave, and they climbed up and caught her in a net and brought her to the village. She died because she longed for human flesh; she refused to eat taro and breadfruit. But before she died, she taught the women to weave.

"A few years ago, a group from Rurutu brought the legend of Hina to Tahiti for Tiurai, and they won the grand prize in the singing and dancing competition. The women love Hina. They cry for her tragedy, because she gave them the knowledge of weaving."

I toured the island of Tubuai with Jacques Drollet, Ingrid's father and the chief administrator of the Australs. Tubuai is small, about six miles long and three miles wide, with a population of 2,000. Jacques and his wife, Fara, had lived there for two years.

"When we first arrived," Jacques said, "Fara and I drove around the island 11 times before we realized that this is all there is."

We drove through tiny villages, past people working in taro patches and fields of potatoes, carrots, and arrowroot, past grazing cattle and rooting pigs. Fishing nets hung in trees by the sea, and outrigger canoes—some with masts, some with motors—were beached on red-sand shores beneath the swinging boughs of casuarina trees.

"The difference between the Austral Islands and Tahiti is that 90 percent of the people here are farmers and fishermen. There is almost no tourism. Time has a different meaning for people here. Eternity lies before them."

Sunday finery brightens the Protestant church in Moerai on the island of Rurutu. Since the arrival of missionaries in the early 1800s, churches have served as focal points of community life in French Polynesia.

Seated on a mat they wove, women of the Rurutu village of Avera make hats and baskets out of the leaves of pandanus—a plant found throughout the Pacific islands. After soaking, the long leaves are draped on trees to dry (below); then the women cut them into strips for weaving (bottom). Widely known for the fine quality of their wares, women of the Austral Islands take pride in their craft and still work in communal groups—the foundation of traditional village life.

We stopped at an agricultural cooperative where people were sacking and weighing potatoes in a cavernous storehouse. "Tubuai and Rurutu have very successful agricultural operations," Jacques explained. "The islands are very green; everything grows easily here. We send the potatoes to Tahiti—I call Tubuai 'the Idaho of the South Seas.' Even so, this business, like so much in French Polynesia, is heavily subsidized by the government—almost 50 percent. France has given the people a high standard of living, but I am concerned about the shift of vital forces from the outer islands to Tahiti. The old people want to live like their parents; the young want to change."

We drove inland along the *ara matua*—the road of the forefathers. "It was luck and unluck that the Polynesians embraced the Europeans so fast," said Jacques. "We have a good life, but we have lost some of our culture. The Polynesian society was in chaos when the Europeans arrived. The people were warring and eating each other. Something had to change. The missionaries were not a completely negative influence, as some have said. The society is a living body, not a museum. It is a good thing that it evolves; otherwise we would be like stones and mountains."

A storm passed over the island. The distant skies were streaked with

Garden of fabric surrounds a young girl attending a festival in Maeva on Huahine. Floral patterns distinguish residents of different island villages competing in various events; wives of 19th-century missionaries introduced the long, loose-fitting dresses, sometimes described as "Mother Hubbards."

softening colors, like pastels bleeding on wet paper. Clouds cast shadows on the sea, moving south, following waves that roll toward Antarctica. Mists rose around Tubuai's ancient volcano, a weathered, green landscape of silk-on-bones hills. No other island was visible on any horizon.

"The islands of Polynesia are small and remote," said Jacques. "Little changes are big here. The Polynesian culture is struggling to survive. I was the chief of the education department for seven years, and during that time we brought the Polynesian language back into the schools. I think that is a great achievement. A language is a living thing that belongs to a people. A culture remains alive if the language lives. If a Tahitian cannot express himself in his own language, then he is a brown-skinned European.

"I think that one of the most fascinating things that could happen here would be to have a trilingual society. People would keep sentimental ties with France, speaking French. They would live in their own culture, speaking Tahitian, and to travel and understand the world that affects them, they would learn English."

We headed back into the main village, passing mailboxes full of fresh loaves of French bread. "Like many Tahitians, I am of two cultures," said Jacques. "My father was European, my mother Tahitian. I look like a big, tall Norwegian, but I live by my Tahitian heart. I think that finally we can live with both worlds—because we must."

Alone in the faraway seas 900 miles southeast of Tahiti—almost touching the Tropic of Capricorn—is a small cluster of isles known as the Gambiers. A single thread of reef and motu arcs around the group, and nearly all of the 600 inhabitants live on the main island, Mangareva, one of the most isolated places in the world.

From the sea, Mangareva looks prehistoric. Its high peak, Mount Duff, is dark and rugged; dense palms trim the shores, always rocking; inland, the soil is black and rich. The lagoon is a jewel of shocking-blue waters—and beneath the surface, in the perfect warmth and turquoise clarity of the tropic sea, thrives the oyster that produces the rare black pearl.

The black pearl is a hallmark of French Polynesia. The oyster, *Pinctada margaritifera*, is found in other warm seas of the world, but if the water is polluted, the oyster will die. It flourishes in lagoons of the Tuamotu atolls and the Gambiers, forming the iridescent gem that is a measure of an environment that is pristine.

Most of the natural black pearls were harvested from the lagoons of the Tuamotus and Gambiers in the past century. In the early 1900s the Japanese perfected methods for culturing pearls, and in the 1970s French Polynesians began to culture black pearls, using the Japanese techniques. After a series of cyclones in 1983 devastated the copra industry, black pearls became the islands' leading commodity. Although the territory imports many more goods than it produces, cultured black pearls hold promise as a valuable developing industry.

One of the pioneers of the cultured black pearl industry is Robert Wan, whose farm in the Gambiers lagoon is the largest in French Polynesia. Robert took Nicholas DeVore and me to his pearl-farm station, a sprawling stilt house in the northern part of the lagoon, where more than two dozen workers were washing and checking oysters.

At the farm, tiny oysters are collected, placed in mesh pouches, and suspended in the lagoon waters from a network of floating rafts. Growing oysters are pulled up and cleaned, and at about the age of three they are ready for seeding. Japanese technicians place a ball of shell and a snip of black mantle tissue into each living oyster; the grafted mantle forms a sac that secretes layers of nacre around the ball, isolating it and creating a pearl. In natural pearls, the entry of the foreign object is accidental. Otherwise, natural and cultured pearls are identical. The seeded oysters are put back in the lagoon, and two years later the pearls are harvested.

"From the beginning, out of one million oysters, 200,000 survive," Robert explained. "Then comes the seeding. Out of every 100 oysters seeded, 25 die and 25 reject the seed. Of the pearls produced by the other 50, most are of poor quality or irregular shape. Only 5 are perfect.

"There are so many aspects to producing a pearl. You must raise the oysters and nurture them at each stage. The Gambiers are ideal for pearls. Few people come here, the oysters are healthier, and there is a pure quality of the water that makes the pearl crystal especially lovely."

Robert showed me a pearl, metallic black, its translucent surface reflecting elusive shades of pink, blue, and green. "Black pearls are so exciting,"

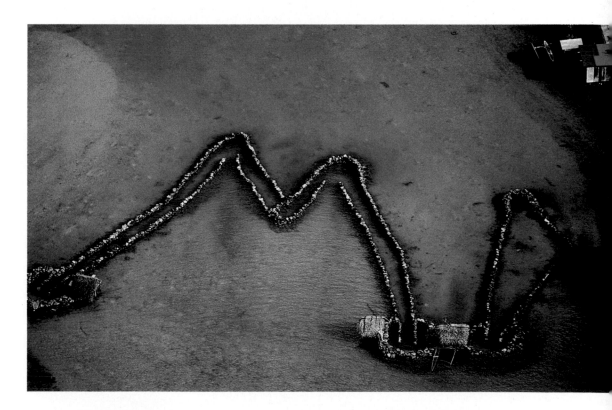

Thousand-year-old village comes to light on Huahine, where archaeologist Yosihiko Sinoto of Honolulu's Bishop Museum washes a fresh find—a canoe bailer. Islanders have used the stone fish traps (above) for five centuries.

FOLLOWING PAGES: *Powdery beaches fringe Aukena, an uninhabited isle in the remote Gambiers. Across the lagoon looms Mount Duff on Mangareva.*

he said. "For all we know about culturing pearls, we don't know exactly what makes the most beautiful ones so perfect. We can't make it happen every time. We do everything right—and finally it is a mystery."

Just north of the Gambiers, the low coral atolls of the Tuamotu Archipelago stretch across the sea for more than a thousand miles in a long, gentle arc. Nearly half of the 78 isles are uninhabited. The Tuamotus are seldom visited; even the Tahitians are curious about them.

I pictured the Tuamotus as quintessential lost isles of the tropics, tiny circles of sand and palms adrift in the remote reaches of the South Seas. When I first flew to French Polynesia, at night, I looked down on the endless black ocean, its surface silvery with the glow of a full moon. Then I spotted a dark ring on the sea—an atoll. One of the Tuamotus. On its shore, a single light shone. I longed for the island.

The largest of the Tuamotus is Rangiroa, a huge oval of more than 200 isles and motu surrounding a lagoon so big that the island of Tahiti—a hundred miles in circumference—could fit inside. Rangiroa is a broken ring of white sand and quaking palms nearly flush with the sea. It is so narrow that from the shore of the lagoon I could hear the surf on the sea side,

French Polynesia's largest cathedral, St. Michel, nestles among palms in the town of Rikitea on Mangareva, an island of fewer than 600 inhabitants. Completed in 1841, the church was built of white coral on the site—and with some of the stones—of an ancient marae. The lavish interior gleams with decorations of mother-of-pearl (right), gathered from the Gambiers lagoon.

Precious strands of black-pearl oysters (left) dangle in mesh pouches at Robert Wan's Tahiti Perles farm off Mangareva. Suspended from rafts around the pearl-farm station (above), seeded oysters remain in the lagoon's warm waters for two years before harvesting. Only one in twenty yield perfect cultured pearls like those modeled by Mere Neti of Tahiti (right).

the booming voice of the barrier reef. In the old days, people here would lash themselves to the trunks of palms, way up high, to ride out storms.

I explored the far lagoon and distant motu of Rangiroa with Gérard Bédé, a young Frenchman who came to the islands of Tahiti 15 years ago, fulfilling a boyhood dream of living in paradise.

"I love the life of freedom," said Gérard. "To live like a wild animal with all this space around me. I love the colors, the sea, the beauty."

We zipped down the lagoon in his small motorboat, to a narrow pass between two islets. It was high tide, when the ocean waters rush through the pass at speeds of more than five knots. Gérard maneuvered the boat into the center of the pass, and we jumped into the water with snorkels on and swept through the pass with the incoming seas, flying above the blue depths. We soared over streaming shoals of wild-colored fish, past looming coral heads, our arms outstretched like Superman's. Sharks lurked near the bottom, eyeing the massing thunderheads of fish that rode the current as we did, floating weightless through blue space.

We took the boat to the far southeast corner of the lagoon, some 40 miles away. There, I walked on a cloud of pink and orange sand, a tiny sandbar set in the banded blues of the dazzling lagoon. Gérard speared fish and cooked them on a grill of coral and shells along the shore of an islet of palms. *"Ah, c'est très, très, très beau,"* said Gérard. "This is simplicity, this is sublime. This is the beauty of the true Polynesia."

We motored out into the open ocean, along the northern shore of the atoll. Breakers swelled and crashed in a turquoise-and-white froth. Dolphins frolicked around the boat, and flying fish leaped from our path like skipping stones. We anchored offshore. "Each time I dive, I am a discoverer," said Gérard. "It's a dream world, but we must live our dreams."

We dived into the ocean. I swam along the undersea cliffs of the atoll. Coral walls plunged into the velvety blue-black emptiness below. Huge fish flippered by, unafraid. Above, the hot eye of the tropic sun burned white, and the warm sea rolled to the far horizon to touch the sky. On Rangiroa, palms bowed in the wind, and white terns wheeled in the air. This was the world that shaped the Polynesians. I rocked with the waves, floating free in the paradise of my imaginings.

Pristine vistas of the blue Pacific stretch to every horizon from the sea-level atoll of Rangiroa, largest of the Tuamotus—a long, curving archipelago of 78 seldom visited isles. A white tern (top) soars above the lagoon, giving expression to the ethereal beauty of French Polynesia.

THE COOK ISLANDS

Among the Tiniest Stars

By Christine Eckstrom Lee
Photographs by Nicholas DeVore III

*E*xham Wichman doesn't like to be called "Mr. Wichman." "That's so embarrassing!" he told me. "We use first names here. We all know each other. If I go to see the prime minister, Tom Davis, I don't say 'Hello, Mr. Prime Minister.' I say, 'Tom! What's happening?'"

Exham's home is Rarotonga, in the Cook Islands, where he drives a colorful open-air tour bus and shows visitors the daily life of people on a faraway tropical isle. "We live in communities," Exham explained. "The Cook Islands are small. We all need each other. There's no poor; there's no rich. It is a peaceful place. If you do something wrong, how are you going to face your community again? We live by the Bible. All the churches preach, 'If there's a heaven somewhere, then it must be here. Let's make our home a heaven.' And so we try."

In the Cook Islands, paradise finds expression both in the South Sea beauty of the land and in the small-town intimacy of the communities. Exham's manner reflects the spirit and charm of the little-known Cooks, 15 volcanic isles and coral atolls sprinkled across the South Pacific between Samoa and Tahiti. They are among the tiniest stars in the Pacific universe. With a total land area of only 93 square miles—about the size of the Massachusetts island of Martha's Vineyard—the Cooks pepper a swath of ocean almost three times as large as Texas. The islands are divided into northern and southern groups. Most of the northern isles are sparsely populated atolls, all but inaccessible to travelers. Nearly 90 percent of the 18,000 inhabitants live on the volcanic islands of the southern group—many of which lie closer to Tahiti than to the northern Cooks.

Unity would seem elusive among such scattered isles, but as I traveled around the southern Cooks, I found ties that bind them together. A woman

Lofty pantry provides Cook Islands children with a Polynesian staple, free for the picking. Mature coconut palms may bear 50 nuts a year for more than half a century, supplying food and drink, oil, utensils, and ornaments.
PRECEDING PAGES: *Day ends on Tekopua, a remote islet in the reef of Aitutaki in the Cooks, themselves a remote, unspoiled part of Polynesia west of Tahiti.*

FLOWER ART: FRANGIPANI *(Plumeria rubra)*

on Rarotonga sent greetings with me to her cousin on Mauke; a man on Mauke gave me a note for his niece on Aitutaki; and from Atiu I brought messages to friends on Rarotonga. In so doing, I became a small part of the informal communications network known as the "coconut wireless," which spreads information with the speed of rumor and is often cited as the source of news.

On these remote islands linked by families, friends, and the coconut wireless, the relatively few tourists are highly visible, even on Rarotonga, the largest island. At first I was surprised when people would ask me, "You are from the United States? Do you know Peggy from San Francisco? Or John from Los Angeles? He comes here every year." Such questions quickly became part of the appeal of a place still so unspoiled that some visitors are remembered by name—first name, of course.

The Cook Islands have historical ties with Samoa, Tahiti, and New Zealand. According to legend, a warrior from Samoa and a navigator from Tahiti met at sea while on voyages of discovery. They sailed together, found Rarotonga, and divided it between them. Many Cook Islanders trace their lineage to Karika, the Samoan, and Tangiia, the Tahitian.

Another tradition holds that around A.D. 1000 an explorer named Kupe, of Tahitian and Cook Islands descent, left the east coast of Rarotonga and journeyed more than 1,800 miles southwest to discover New Zealand. Voyaging between Rarotonga and New Zealand increased, and over the next several centuries Cook Islanders and Tahitians gradually settled the southern point of the Polynesian triangle. In language and culture, Cook Islanders remain close to the Tahitians and to the Maoris of New Zealand.

*T*he European discovery of the Cooks took place slowly, from the 16th to the early 19th century. Some islands were sighted or visited, then misplaced on maps and rediscovered years later. Since that time, the islands named for Captain Cook—who found five of the southern ones—have fared somewhat differently than most of their Polynesian neighbors.

The Cooks were too small to be aggressively sought by the 19th-century colonial powers; even Captain Cook called them "detached parts of the earth." Made a protectorate by Great Britain in 1888 and annexed by New Zealand in 1901, the Cook Islands became self-governing in free association with New Zealand in 1965. Cook Islanders manage their internal affairs, but they have New Zealand citizenship, and New Zealand provides defense and economic aid. The partnership is friendly; more than 20,000 Cook Islanders live and work in New Zealand, and many of the visitors to the Cooks are New Zealanders on holiday.

More than half of the Cooks' population lives on Rarotonga, but the island never seems crowded or busy. Often described as a "miniature Tahiti," Rarotonga is a round volcanic isle of 25 square miles, its center a jungle-green realm of serrated ridges and 2,000-foot peaks with eroded rock tips pointing to the sky. Clouds billow and swirl around them as if blown by the mountains themselves. The villages cluster on the narrow coastal plain encircling the island. From the shore, the low thunder of breakers on the reef sounds like the rumble of a distant train. The lonely reaches of the Pacific extend to every horizon, unrelieved by sight of land.

Avarua, the capital and administrative center, is just a bit larger than

Rarotonga's other villages. The town is quiet and shady; more people stroll than drive cars. By law, no building is taller than a coconut palm. Outrigger canoes are beached by the sea, and occasionally a stray chicken dashes across the road. The pace is languid; even government officials don't always feel obliged to wear coats and ties and shoes. The outside world is out there somewhere. My first morning on Rarotonga, I turned on the radio to hear the announcer say, "And now for the news. Due to poor reception from New Zealand, there is no news today."

Since 1974, when Rarotonga's airstrip was expanded to accommodate jets, tourism has grown and now plays an increasingly important role in the economy of the Cooks, which have few natural resources. At the modest Cook Islands Tourist Authority building in Avarua, I spoke with marketing manager Dorice Reid, a lovely, graceful woman with a red hibiscus in her hair. A Cook Islander, Dorice returned home after living and working in New Zealand for 30 years—a reversal of the migration trend from smaller islands to bigger ones that is occurring throughout the Pacific.

"I love this island. I'll never leave again," she told me. "Living in New Zealand, I realized that I didn't know my home any more. I can trace my ancestors back to the first two canoes that arrived on Rarotonga. I wanted to live in my country and work with the people here. The Cook Islands are changing right now, and my concern for the growth in tourism is that it doesn't exceed the capability of the people and the islands to cope with the changes. We must manage tourism to protect what is unique here. Our people and our way of life are our national treasures."

I saw something of that way of life when I toured Rarotonga with Exham Wichman. We drove along the island's west coast and around Exham's home village of Arorangi. In a morning we traveled about three miles, pausing every few hundred yards at community buildings, homes, taro patches, and orange groves while Exham offered lively observations on Cook Islands living.

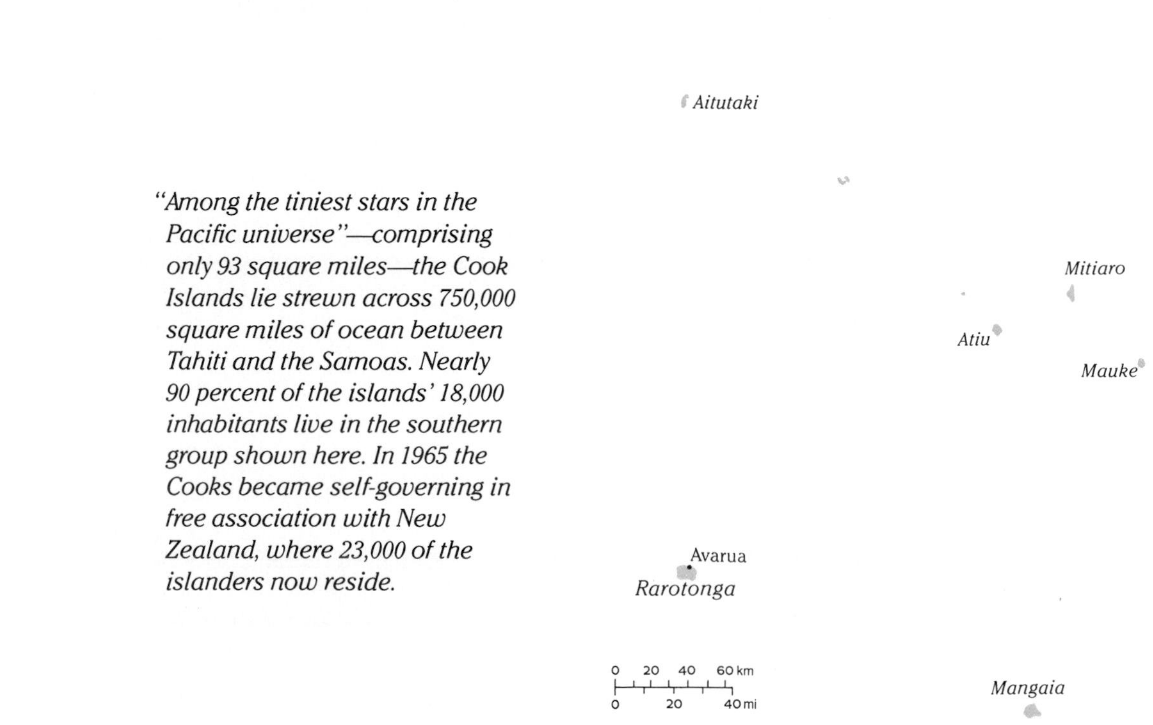

Palmerston
Atoll

ʃ Aitutaki

"Among the tiniest stars in the Pacific universe"—comprising only 93 square miles—the Cook Islands lie strewn across 750,000 square miles of ocean between Tahiti and the Samoas. Nearly 90 percent of the islands' 18,000 inhabitants live in the southern group shown here. In 1965 the Cooks became self-governing in free association with New Zealand, where 23,000 of the islanders now reside.

Mitiaro

Atiu

Mauke

Avarua
Rarotonga

0   20   40   60 km

0   20   40 mi

Mangaia

We stopped before a typical house—one-story, concrete, tin-roofed—set among trees and flowers. "How do those people live in that house?" asked Exham. "You don't have to go inside to see how. It's all out there in front of you. When you look at those trees and other plants you say, 'That's bush.' No. That's the supermarket. All the trees have a purpose."

He waved his hand at an avocado tree. "That tree tells us they have a pig; avocado pears are pig food. When I look at an avocado, I see pork.

"The coconut palms mean they have eggs and poultry to eat. Coconut feeds the chickens. Look at a coconut and see a nice fat chicken."

He pointed to a large tree with no leaves. "That's a kapok. It supplies your mattress. One mattress per tree per year. The mango, breadfruit, grapefruit, and orange trees will bear fruit for more than a lifetime. Just plant a tree and you'll never see the end of the food."

We drove along the seaside road. "You can't eat pigs and chickens all the time," said Exham. "So you must learn the art of fishing. Fish have roadways. You learn where they go, put a net across their track, and bring the lot home."

Just beyond the white breakers roaring on the reef, a humpback whale emerged from the sea like a slow-motion rocket, shedding sheets of water, twisting gracefully as it cleared the surface and crashed back into the ocean with a concussive splash. More whales burst from the sea, and we watched them blow, flip their tails, and perform gargantuan acrobatics.

"We don't usually see them so close to shore," Exham said. "But we hear them at night. Boom! Right out of the water. Boom! We don't bother the whales. They are part of the mystery of the sea."

In the late 18th and early 19th centuries, whalers, traders, and missionaries sailed into the seas around the Pacific isles, following close behind the European explorers—and discovering a few islands themselves. Whalers and traders generally preferred the larger islands—Hawaii, Tahiti, New Zealand. But for the missionaries, no island with souls to save was too small to visit. When the missionaries arrived in the Cooks in the 1820s, the islanders embraced Christianity so quickly and with such zeal that some became missionaries themselves, spreading the faith to other isles.

The Reverend John Williams of the London Missionary Society is often credited with the discovery of Rarotonga in 1823, although the island was probably visited in 1789 by the *Bounty* mutineers. Williams brought with him a Polynesian missionary named Papeiha, from the Tahitian island of Raiatea. Like the Tahitians, the Cook Islanders had looked to Raiatea as Havai'i, the spiritual homeland of their ancestors. In Cook Islands mythology, Rarotonga was once attached to the south side of Raiatea. Long ago, the Raiateans killed two Rarotongan priests who were bringing tribute to Raiatea's high altar; in response, the angry gods carried Rarotonga and its people to safety far away to the south.

Regular voyaging between Tahiti and Rarotonga had stopped centuries before the arrival of John Williams, but when he came ashore with Papeiha, one of the first questions the Cook Islanders asked the Raiatean was why his people had killed the Rarotongan priests, causing their island to be moved far away. In fact, Williams had set sail in search of Rarotonga because he had heard the same legend from an old priest on Raiatea.

Williams left Papeiha on Rarotonga, and when he returned four years later, the people had been converted to Christianity. The old hand of the traditional social structure fit neatly into the new glove of the church hierarchy. Settlements with chiefs and family elders were replaced by villages with ministers and deacons. During much of the 19th century, the London Missionary Society regulated life in the Cooks with the authority of a government, uniting the people through a common faith and helping to keep the islands in native hands. The L.M.S. divided Rarotonga into five villages, with a church at the center of each. Although other faiths are now represented, most people belong to the Cook Islands Christian Church established by the first missionaries, and island life revolves around the churches and their surrounding communities.

I attended church one Sunday in the village of Titikaveka on the south shore of Rarotonga. A tolling bell summoned the congregation, and the streets were filled with hundreds of people walking to the stately coral-and-limestone church, built in 1835. Fresh flowers and potted plants adorned the altar, and in the corner where the children sat wiggling and squirming in their pews, there were tables covered with gleaming rugby trophies won by various community teams.

With a hefty digging stick, island official Joe Herman prepares holes for taro shoots in his plot on Rarotonga; palm leaves form a mulch around them. Six-month-old plants behind Joe will yield edible roots in another six.

FOLLOWING PAGES: *Verdant forests clothe the hills of Rarotonga. The name of the islands honors Capt. James Cook, who visited several of them in the 1770s.*

137

During the service, the choirs sang both Protestant hymns and Polynesian 'īmene—the former with sweetness, the latter with gusto. The men, dressed in black and white, stood together and sang as one bold voice, rocking back and forth in time with the 'īmene. Across from them, the women, in delicate, wide-brimmed woven hats and bright floral dresses, answered the men's singing with airy soprano harmonies. Through the pastel-colored windows, flowering bushes and palm trees bowed in the wind, as if in swaying rhythm with the songs.

After the service, the minister invited the congregation and visitors to the large meeting hall across the street for "some coffee and some food." "Food" was a banquet of island dishes spread across a long table half the length of the hall. The scene was a combination of a Baptist church supper in the American South and a traditional Polynesian feast. There were platters and bowls of chicken, potato salad, coleslaw, and homemade biscuits, along with taro, breadfruit, and papaya.

Dr. Teariki Matenga, a cabinet minister in the Cook Islands government and a speaker for the church, encouraged the visitors to fill their plates and enjoy a nice Sunday dinner. Afterward, the congregation ate, and Dr. Matenga gave a brief speech thanking the visitors for coming to the church. Some of us stood up and responded. "This is the warmest, happiest place I have ever seen," a New Zealander said. An American said, "If the whole world was more like the Cook Islands, it would be a much more peaceful place for us all to live."

*I*n the Cook Islands, community pride runs strong. On Saturday afternoons in Avarua, rugby matches between neighboring villages seem to bring out the entire island population to cheer for favorite teams. Friendly rivalries between islands are a natural extension of the competitive community spirit. People told me what other isles of the southern Cooks were known for, as if challenging any island to outdo them. I heard that Aitutaki has the best dancers and bananas, and the prettiest lagoon; Mangaia raises the sweetest pineapples; Atiu is famous for its flying fish and secret caves; the wood-carvers of Mitiaro make the finest outrigger canoes; and perhaps the most beautiful women in the Cooks come from Mauke.

I flew to Mauke with photographer Nicholas DeVore to catch a freighter traveling among the southern Cooks. As our small plane left Rarotonga, I saw white mist rising from the lace skirt of breakers encircling the island. Beyond the reef, the water was so clear that I could see where the undersea base of Rarotonga descends into the dark blue deep.

On Mauke, our hosts Tara and Kura Purea greeted us at the airstrip with kisses and flower leis (called 'ei in the Cooks). The inter-island freighter was due the following morning; I learned its importance to the islanders when Kura asked me—right after her warm hello—"By any chance, did you bring bread? Oh, we are dying for bread. We have had no boat in almost two months, and the whole island is out of flour."

No one had suggested to me that bread might be a lovely gift to bring to

Coral necklace rims the lagoon and motu—*islets—of the Aitutaki group. An ancient volcano subsided here, leaving bits and pieces of land within the reef. Some call Aitutaki's broad lagoon the Pacific's most beautiful.*

Mauke, and I was especially touched that evening when Tara and Kura served fresh homemade biscuits with dinner: They had saved a last bit of flour to make them for their guests.

Tara and Kura both teach at the public school on Mauke, an island of about 800 people, half of them schoolchildren. Tara used to be the chief administrative officer of Mauke, and before that he taught school on Rarotonga and on Manihiki in the northern Cooks. Kura told me of a trip they once made to Australia. "One moment I remember well was when we stopped at King's Cross in the middle of Sydney and watched the people rushing by. It was something to see them all running at once, not even looking at each other. No one rushes here, and we always say hello."

That night, from my pandanus-roofed bungalow by the sea, I could hear

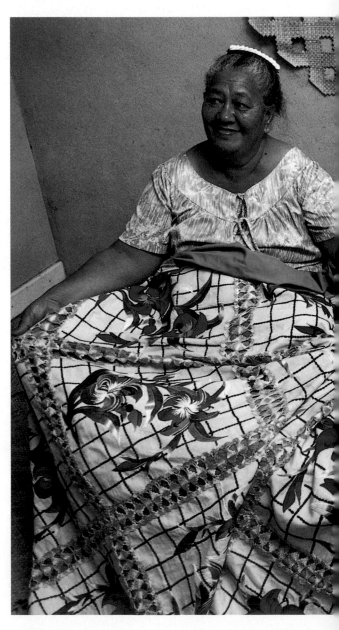

Nature's flowers reappear in Cook Islands quilts. Hibiscus (upper) and heliconia splash color in gardens, and Rarotonga women—Mrs. Willie Katuke, Mrs. Parau Taruia, and "Mama" Ruta Tixier—display their handiwork. Missionary wives taught the skill to islanders, who combined patchwork with appliqué and embroidery.

the surf on the reef. The bungalow nestled in a grove of coconut palms, and above the tossing fronds the sky was jeweled with stars. The Southern Cross, hallmark of the South Pacific heavens, shone near the heart of the Milky Way. Reflected starlight cast a pale white sheen on the night world, and I found it hard to close my eyes to the glow.

When the freighter appeared offshore the following morning, most of the men of Mauke went down to the landing to help unload cargo. In wooden rowboats they ferried to shore the goods and supplies that modern Mauke needs but cannot produce: diesel fuel, kerosene, tinned meat, rice, sugar, coffee, tea, soap, powdered milk, cooking oil, cigarettes, cabin bread, and, finally, flour.

When Nicholas and I boarded the freighter, we discovered we were the

only passengers. Tara and Kura had told me that on islands with air service no one wants to take the freighter any more. "If someone offered to pay me to take the boat," said Kura, "I would refuse!"

The Cook Islands freighter was named the *Mataora*, which means "happy," and she was headed north to Mitiaro, then northwest to Aitutaki. She was small, but the seas were calm, and the cook, a young Rarotongan named Miri, prepared meals that would have pleased a restaurant customer.

Lance, the chief engineer, a large, square-set man from Aitutaki with a hearty laugh, told me stories of warfare between the islands of the southern Cooks in premissionary times. "The islands were always raiding each other—for women, revenge, different reasons," he said as we sat around the table after dinner. "Aitutaki would eat Mitiaro, Mitiaro would eat Mauke, and Atiu ate everybody. We ate a few Europeans, too." After that, Lance would encourage me to eat more at meals, and sometimes when he walked by he would pinch my forearm and say, "Not ready yet!"

Late the first night the engines slowed; we had reached Mitiaro, and the freighter was idling offshore until dawn. I peeked out the porthole for a glimpse of the island and saw two men in white with long poles in their hands, seemingly standing on the water. Moving slowly across the surface, the figures faded in and out of sight. They were fishermen in small outrigger canoes, but they looked like the ghosts of the ancestors.

In the morning, I went ashore in a rowboat, wedged between huge sacks of potatoes with two baby goats in my lap. While the cargo was being unloaded, I wandered around the cluster of villages by the landing, where most of Mitiaro's 300 residents live. Fifteen outrigger canoes, the pride of local wood-carvers, were lined up near the landing.

A woman named Tearoa Makara introduced herself and invited me to her home for coffee. As the community development officer for the island, Tearoa organizes activities for the women and encourages them to make baskets and other wares to sell on Rarotonga. Long strips of pandanus lay drying on the ground beside her house and, out back, five members of her family were preparing arrowroot in the traditional way: Her mother-in-law and auntie washed and peeled the roots; her husband—the island constable—and his brother-in-law grated the roots; and Tearoa's niece washed the gratings with water, squeezing white juice from the arrowroot through a cloth. The fine sediment that settles out from the water is dried in the sun for a month before it is ready for use in cooking.

"In your country, you have machines for everything," said Tearoa. "Here, all of our work is by hand." Inside their house, handwoven pandanus mats covered the floors. There were colorful embroidered and appliquéd pillows on the beds and chairs and an array of dainty hats on the walls, all made by Tearoa.

"This is what ladies in the Cook Islands do," she said. "Weaving and other crafts provide us with extra income. Mitiaro has no real exports, so the boat sometimes comes only once every three months or so. We have a little shop here, but in three months' time all the goods are gone, and the people go back to the arrowroot and the banana, back to the land."

For the journey from Mitiaro to Aitutaki, the *Mataora*'s crew hoisted her huge brown sails, and the vessel became, in the words of Captain Tig Loe, "a mizzen-rigged schooner-freighter." Our speed increased to ten knots as we motor-sailed to Aitutaki, 140 miles away.

We arrived in the dark and circled offshore. Squalls swept in, and at dawn, under skies still swirling with black clouds, we saw the sad toll of the stormy night: a beautiful 46-foot ketch aground on the reef. Passengers and crew were safely ashore. Captain Tig shook his head. "It's a part of life around here. The waters are tricky. It can happen to anyone."

Polynesian legends tell many tales of islands found by voyagers blown off course, of canoes lost at sea, of prayers for successful ocean journeys. The ancient navigator Ru is said to have discovered Aitutaki after losing his way in a storm.

Sunday afternoons on Aitutaki are peaceful. About 2,500 people live on the island, a hilly green land with a broad, clear lagoon and a necklace of *motu*—islets—with sugary beaches. I drove around on a scooter and saw women in their churchgoing finery, boys playing marbles in the streets, and people picnicking in front of their homes. Only the Seventh-day Adventists worked, having had their day of rest on Saturday.

I met a Seventh-day Adventist, Taamo Charlie, working in his potato patch. Nearby, two of his eighteen children flew homemade plastic kites in a field of arrowroot. He was planning to send some of his bananas on the *Mataora* the next day for export to Samoa. Like many Cook Islanders, Taamo Charlie has more than one job. He farms his land to feed his family, and works at Aitutaki's water plant for extra money. "I've been to New Zealand," he said. "There you must buy everything—even food! Mangoes, bananas—everything! I work at the water plant, but with eighteen children I'm not worried about the money. I'm just worried about the food."

The *Mataora* left Aitutaki for Samoa—with Taamo Charlie's bananas on board—and I flew south to Atiu, an island of 10 square miles and some

Hard aground, the 46-foot ketch Manureva *lies helpless on Aitutaki's reef. In these same waters, Captain Cook encountered squally weather and "sharp Coral rocks, so that anchoring would be attended with . . . danger."*

Seagoing lifeline, the Mataora *(opposite) anchors off Mauke Island in the Cooks. Cargo, loaded into a lighter (left) and ferried ashore, makes a welcome pile at the landing (below). Residents of the isolated isles depend on the freighter for supplies. The* Mataora *cruises among the southern Cooks, completing a circuit every month or so. She carries fuel and food but few passengers. Islanders today prefer the convenience of flight to the romance of ocean travel.*

1,200 people. In contrast to the other southern Cooks, Atiu's villages are grouped in the middle of the island, an area of rolling, red-soil terrain; from there the island tapers down to fertile lowlands. Between the lowlands and a narrow fringing reef lies a wide, rugged ring of ancient uplifted coral known as the *makatea;* a woman on Atiu told me the makatea was "the land God made first."

Dense with underbrush and trees, the jagged makatea shields the island's interior from the sea like a boot-camp obstacle course. Underground, the ancient coral is honeycombed with tunnels and caves—the source of Atiu legends.

I hiked across the makatea to Atiu's most famous cave, Anatakitaki. Two young men of the island, Kau Henry and Taio Kautai, guided me there with Nicholas and Pat and Ian Crysell of New Zealand. The walk was rough and slow, but the forest was shady and aflutter with birds. The ground outside the cave was carpeted with ferns and low palms, and vines draped the entrance. We climbed down into a large hole.

With lanterns to light our path, we wound through the cave, crawling through narrow passages to yawning rooms toothy with stalactites and stalagmites. We entered a chamber deep in the cave and heard a click.

Coral heads stud the lagoon of Aitutaki, where an islander spears fish for an evening meal. In precontact Polynesia, fruit trees and a bountiful coral reef could supply nearly all an island's needs. Corals, which survive best in warm, shallow waters, have kept pace here with a subsiding volcano, building both the jagged limestone clumps and the encircling reef.

"Ah, we are lucky," said Kau. "They are here." More clicks increased to a staccato, and near the roof of the cave tiny objects were darting and swooping. They were *kopeka*—swiftlets—little birds that nest high in the cave and make clicking sounds when they fly about in the darkness. They leave the cave mostly at night; it is said that once outside they never alight. At dawn they return to Anatakitaki.

Kau and Taio led us to the cave's other entrance, a small round hole in the roof. Sunlight made a pool on the floor. There, Kau told us the legend of the kopeka and the cave of Anatakitaki:

"Long ago on a full-moon night, when the men go fishing and there is also dancing, a man had a fight with his wife because she went dancing while he was fishing. The wife ran away in the night. She came to the makatea and found this cave, where she stayed hidden a long time. The kopeka befriended her and went with her when she searched for food. One day the husband was working in his field and he heard a bird in a tree, calling to him. He followed the bird from tree to tree until finally he reached the cave. His wife was waiting for him there, and they made peace."

Later, people stayed in the caves of Atiu in time of war. "My ancestors lived here before the missionaries came," Kau said. "The missionaries moved all the families to one place in the interior, under one God."

Kau spoke of a light called *te rongo,* still seen on the *marae,* or temple platforms. "It is a sign that a chief will die. It flies from one marae to another. I have seen te rongo, just before a chief died. It looks like a falling star."

*L*egends remembered and retold carry island traditions to each new generation. On a beach on Rarotonga, I watched a group of young dancers tell stories in the lyrical style expressive of the Polynesian love of life.

The group, called Karioi—Entertainment, is composed of nearly 50 teenage girls and boys from the village of Tupapa. "Everyone learns to dance in school when they are very young," said Raui Moetaua, the group's choreographer. "We compose the dances from a story or maybe just a feeling. Some of the dances are traditional and some are new ones we have created. We do it for the fun," she said, "and to be together."

The sky blazed with sunset colors as the dancers performed on the beach at Black Rock, a massive boulder where, legend says, souls departed for the afterlife journey back to the homeland of Havai'i.

Karioi danced to the setting sun, with joyous song, to the beat of drums. They danced a prayer to the god Tangaroa, asking him to guide a canoe safely from Aitutaki to Rarotonga; they sang a sweet 'īmene based on the Song of Solomon. Strumming ukuleles, they sat on the sloping sides of Black Rock, swaying together as they sang, facing the western sea.

A pretty young dancer, Kura Kaveei, her hair shiny with coconut oil and crowned with pink frangipani blossoms, walked over to me and put her 'ei of pink flowers around my neck. "You are from the United States?" she asked. "Oh, so far away." Then she said, with a knowledge of the magic of her land, "I think that when you go home, all this will be a dream."

Costumed in ti *leaves and frangipani blossoms, Fenny Manavaroa dances on Rarotonga. Like the Hawaiian hula, vibrant dances of the Cooks tell stories and reflect the islanders' love of music, motion, and color.*

HAWAII

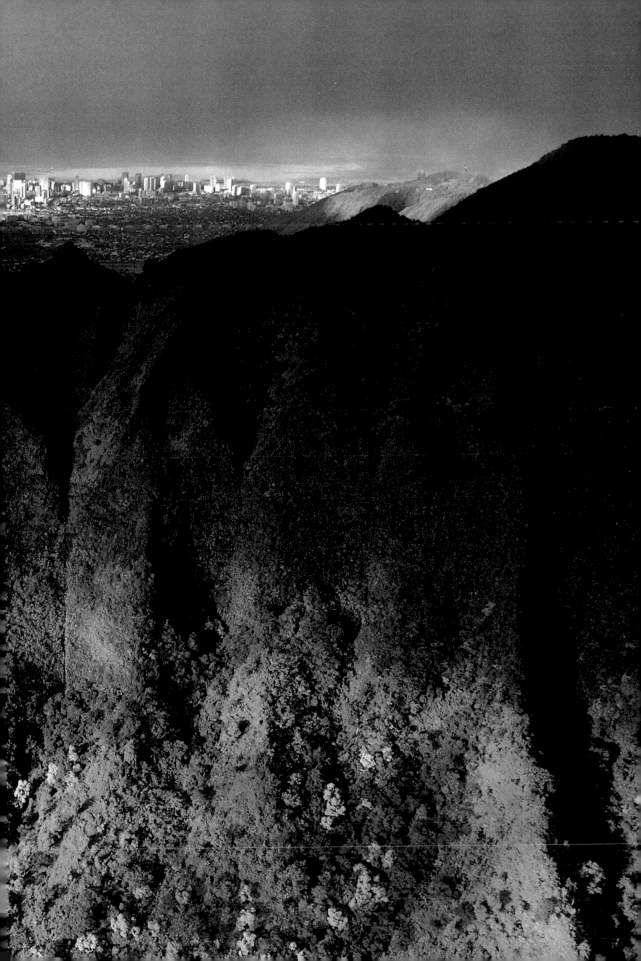

America's Paradise Isles

By Ron Fisher
Photographs by Paul Chesley

I dreamed I was in an airplane buffeted by wild winds. As we lurched and wobbled toward a landing, I exerted every ounce of body English I had, trying to straighten us out. The ground came up, and we fishtailed alarmingly. I awoke in my bunk aboard a rolling cruise ship in the Pacific.

It was dark in my windowless cabin, so I dressed and went out on deck. Astern, dawn was just breaking. The rising sun turned the edges of a huge, seemingly solid bank of clouds pink, then, as I watched, ripped it to shreds. Streaks of orange and red shot into the sky, as if from a distant burning continent. I turned and faced the bow. There, dimly lit by the inferno behind me, a mountainous island rose darkly from the sea, its fringes washed by white, frothy surf. Mist and forest obscured its slopes, and clouds, just beginning to catch the light, sat atop its peaks. Palm trees drooped on the beach, and boats bobbed in a harbor. I wondered: Am I still dreaming, or is this paradise?

It was Kauai, one of the Hawaiian Islands.

For a week I was one of 700 passengers aboard the S.S. *Constitution* as she plied the blue waters of Hawaii. And what better way to first see the islands than from the ocean, as the Polynesian voyagers and European explorers did? Most of our days were warm and sunny, and nights were spent aboard ship, gently rocked by the broad Pacific swells. From the sea in the daytime, the islands looked uninhabited, with no sign of man or his works; but one night we steamed past Honolulu, and the lights of the city twinkled and climbed the inland mountains of Oahu, interrupted by the black bulk of Diamond Head.

During that week we stopped briefly at several of the islands and went ashore to explore.

Timeless symbol of hope arcs above the Hawaiian island of Kauai, nicknamed the Garden Isle. Voyagers from the Marquesas, some 2,000 miles to the south, probably made this their first landfall about 1,200 years ago. PRECEDING PAGES: *Fluted face of the Nuuanu Pali—a heavily eroded, 1,200-foot escarpment—rises inland from Honolulu, dimly glimpsed on Oahu's coast.*

FLOWER ART: HIBISCUS *(Hibiscus saintjohnianus)*

On Kauai we boarded buses and toured what the Hawaiians call the Garden Isle. Geologically the oldest of the inhabited Hawaiian Islands, Kauai has aged somewhat like Arizona, even to possessing its own "Grand Canyon"—a 3,000-foot-deep, 14-mile-long chasm called Waimea. Standing on its rim, we watched red-tailed tropic birds swooping in its arid depths, and heard wild goats bleating on its flanks. Kauai was where Capt. James Cook first came ashore in 1778. The Hawaiians mistook him for a god and honored him accordingly. Kauai also claims the world's "rainiest spot"—Mount Waialeale, where an average of 460 inches falls each year.

On Oahu we gaped at Waikiki Beach and visited the memorial in Pearl Harbor that honors the Americans who perished aboard the U.S.S. *Arizona* during the Japanese attack on December 7, 1941. Intriguing to me were the great crowds of Japanese tourists also visiting the memorial. So many Japanese come that tour-boat announcements over the loudspeaker are in both English and Japanese, and the brochure handed out by the National Park Service is available in two versions as well.

We steamed around little Lanai, largely a pineapple plantation, and Molokai, once a prison for victims of leprosy and only now being developed for tourism.

On Maui we marveled at one of the world's largest banyan trees, a sprawling giant that shades nearly an entire city block. A bus took us, panting in the heat, to the verdant 'Iao Valley to see its famous Needle, a 2,250-foot-tall lava monolith. Maui is shaped like a Ping-Pong paddle, each end formed by a volcano. It is also the site of the Lahainaluna School, the oldest high school west of the Rocky Mountains, founded in 1831.

On the Big Island, Hawaii, we stopped first at Hilo on the east coast. Banyan Drive, lined with trees planted by famous people—Amelia Earhart and "Babe" Ruth, among others—runs past the hotels. From there a bus took us south and up, to Hawaii Volcanoes National Park, where steam and acrid gases leak from the ground. "The smell of sulphur is strong, but not unpleasant to a sinner," wrote Mark Twain after visiting the area in 1866. At Kailua on Hawaii's Kona, or leeward, coast we anchored out a mile or so and went ashore in a large launch, the *Captain Cook.* At dockside a Hawaiian boy, with snorkel, face mask, and flippers, was working the passengers. We'd toss him a quarter, he'd dive for it. He stored the coins in his cheeks like a chipmunk as he dog-paddled near the boat. In the mountains above the harbor, in a drizzle, we negotiated rain-darkened highways past coffee plantations and macadamia nut and orchid farms.

*I*t was while aboard ship that I realized that Hawaii is the only state in the Union that you can sail *among.* Our newest, fourth smallest, and most remote state, Hawaii is a long string of 132 islands, reefs, and shoals stretching across about 1,500 miles of ocean at the northern apex of the Polynesian triangle; it has a total land area of 6,425 square miles. Alaska reaches a little farther west, but Hawaii is our southernmost state, lying on roughly the same latitude as Hong Kong and Mexico City. Of the eight large islands, only seven are inhabited. The smallest of the eight, Kahoolawe, has been used as a bombing target by the U. S. Navy since World War II. Discovery of a number of archaeological sites on Kahoolawe has led to protests against the bombing, and civil suits have compelled the Navy to make an archaeological survey of the island. Niihau, the second smallest, is privately owned. Near the northern end of the string are the Midway Islands, administered by the Navy.

The Hawaiian Islands are volcanic in origin, the summits of an oceanic ridge rising as high as 32,000 feet from the seafloor. Geologists say they may have been formed as the Pacific crustal plate gradually drifted northwest over a hot spot—a source of magma far below the earth's crust that has been producing volcanoes for at least 70 million years. As the plate moved over the hot spot, one island after another appeared. Thus the oldest and most eroded islands are at the northwestern end of the chain, and the newest are in the southeast. In fact, the Big Island of Hawaii is still growing, as Kilauea and Mauna Loa in Hawaii Volcanoes National Park occasionally erupt and add hundreds of acres of new lava to the island.

After a week aboard the *Constitution*—a week of overeating, oversleeping, and overdoing—I jumped ship and went exploring on my own.

On the one hand, I found, Hawaii is simply another state, like Iowa or North Carolina. On the other hand, clinging to it are the remnants of an exotic and "foreign" past. Somerset Maugham wrote of Honolulu: "It is the meeting place of East and West. The very new rubs shoulders with the immeasurably old." Hawaii has its shopping malls and crabgrass, its Woolworths and Safeways, its traffic jams and jetports. But it also has its macadamia nut farms and banyan trees, its ancient gods and legends, and remnants of its lovely, liquid language, full of "aha's" and "ooloo's." It is a genuinely multiracial state, and the Japanese and Chinese in its population give it a decidedly Oriental flavor.

Despite the familiarity of much that you see in Hawaii, there are still some surprises. For instance, in addition to regular holidays such as Christmas and the Fourth of July, Hawaii officially celebrates Prince Kuhio Day, Kamehameha Day, and, instead of Columbus Day, Discoverers' Day.

Hawaii has no resident sea gulls, no commercial billboards, and only one species of land snake. Attempts to establish a permanent sea gull population have so far proved unsuccessful. As for billboards, in 1927 the Outdoor Circle, Hawaii's first women's club, got legislation passed banning

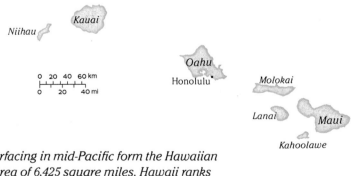

Volcanic peaks surfacing in mid-Pacific form the Hawaiian Islands. With an area of 6,425 square miles, Hawaii ranks as our fourth smallest state. Some four million vacationers arrive each year, many to bask on renowned beaches.

them, so the state's 4,000 miles of highways are free of business advertising. And the snake is a blind, harmless creature much like a big worm.

Hawaii is the only state that grows commercial crops of coffee, macadamia nuts, and pineapples.

It's also the only state where men's shirts are an art form. At first, Hawaiian shirts featured fairly authentic Polynesian designs, but they've become more and more colorful over the years. Celebrities and at least one President—Harry Truman—have appeared in them, and today businessmen and TV newsmen in Honolulu traditionally wear them on Fridays.

There are twice as many Wongs in the Honolulu phone book as there are Smiths. And maps in the front of the telephone directories show which coastal areas will be inundated during a *tsunami,* or seismic sea wave.

Hawaii imports about ten million tons of cargo each year. Virtually every lawn mower and microwave oven, every box of cereal and bottle of A.1. sauce arrives by ship.

The Hawaiian language, melodious as it is, causes some problems. In the early 1800s the missionaries devised a written language for the islands, using just 12 letters—the five vowels and the consonants h, k, l, m, n, p, and w. Consequently, people complain, Hawaiian words seem to be all vowels, and they all look alike. When spoken, however, combinations of vowels often contain glottal stops, and vowel sounds may be short or long. Still, when I'm asked if I've been to Lualualei Beach or Wawahiwaʻa Point, I have to stop and think.

*H*awaii is an endlessly fascinating place, with nooks of Polynesia and crannies of California, but what most interested me about it, and what truly sets it apart from other states, is its past.

Born of volcanic violence, settled by Polynesian voyagers, colonized by assorted races, and harvested—of fortunes and souls—by sundry merchants and missionaries, the islands today are the product of a turbulent history, one with disparate parts.

Part one belongs to the Polynesians. Flying to Hawaii from the mainland, we droned above a changeless sea for hour after hour, thousands of miles with not a hint of a landmark. When the flight attendant made her little speech—"The captain has begun our descent into Honolulu"—and when, a few minutes later, we did indeed land at Honolulu, I marveled at the ease and accuracy of modern navigation, pinpointing these tiny islands in such a vast ocean. But, I realized later, a thousand times more impressive were the navigational skills of the ancient Polynesians. Guided by the waves and the stars, bits of flotsam, and an occasional bird, they found their way across a trackless world that must have seemed as endless to them as outer space seems to us.

The first of them apparently arrived fairly recently in human history, probably about 1,200 years ago. They came from the Marquesas Islands, impelled perhaps by war, perhaps by a shortage of land, or perhaps simply by a desire to wander. Later—about A.D. 1300—another group of settlers evidently arrived, this time from Tahiti. There even may have been round-trip voyages between Tahiti and Hawaii, though scholars are not certain.

On Oahu there is a place where the different Polynesian life-styles are presented for the visitor's inspection. The Polynesian Cultural Center is a

42-acre "living museum" established by the Latter-day Saints in conjunction with the Hawaii campus of Utah's Brigham Young University. Little villages in the styles of Samoa, New Zealand, Fiji, Tahiti, the Marquesas, Tonga, and Hawaii have been built beside a long, narrow lagoon. Students from the various islands, in native costume, demonstrate their crafts and customs, songs and dances beneath waving palm trees.

At the Samoan village a young man was about to begin a fire-making demonstration. "Good afternoon," he said to the assembled crowd. "Welcome to Samoa. In my country, the word of greeting is *tālofa*. Can you say it?" We all chorused, "Ta-LOW-fah." "Far out!" he said.

I strolled for an afternoon with the crowds through the center's villages, past thatched structures—chiefs' houses, meetinghouses, family houses. I tasted poi (bland), danced a Tahitian dance (awkwardly), and went for a canoe ride on the lagoon (hot).

Perhaps the most poignant of the villages was the Hawaiians', for this museum displays only a few examples of the culture of the ancient, pre-contact islanders. I felt their presence, though, on several islands I visited, and most strongly on the little island of Lanai.

Lloyd Cockett, a native, took me for a bumpy, dusty ride in his pickup

Knee-deep in ooze, Alan Tasaka and his family harvest taro from their plot on Kauai. Polynesian voyagers brought the plant here; some islanders still cook and pound the roots to make poi—a dish rich in carbohydrates.

FOLLOWING PAGES: *Roadless and remote, northwestern Kauai's Na Pali coast offers campers secluded tent sites and fog-laden breezes fresh from the sea.*

down to the southernmost tip of Lanai, where the ancient village of Kaunolu sits in the harsh sun. The Hawaiians used chunks of black lava to build the hundred or so structures whose tumbled walls remain, many with petroglyphs chiseled into them. The ruins of a massive *heiau*—temple—sit at the village's highest point, overlooking the sea. "Kamehameha liked to come here to fish," said Lloyd, and I thought at first I must have misunderstood him. A king, gone fishing? Kamehameha the Great, a remarkable man by any country's standards, waged war on rival chiefs in the late 1700s and unified the islands into a single kingdom. "Kings fish, too," said Lloyd.

The future king was a young man when Capt. James Cook stepped ashore on the island of Kauai in January 1778. The Englishman's visit spelled the beginning of the end for the Hawaiian kingdom that Kamehameha was about to establish.

Waimea, the little town on the bay where Cook anchored, today slumbers beneath a brutal sun. It has the aspect of a town that has had one too many traumatic things happen to it: Captain Cook landed here; the island's first missionaries landed here; even Russians landed here. The remains of a fort built by a Russian agent in the early 1800s stand on the point where the Waimea River runs into the bay.

I asked a youth at a gas station how to reach the bay. "Take your first right turn before the bridge," he said, in the tone of someone who's been asked the same question countless times. I soon found myself in a small park beside the river. A black sandspit had built up across the river's mouth, and I stood on it and gazed at the bay, imagining Cook's ships—the *Resolution* and the *Discovery*—at anchor, their longboats filled with sailors and marines coming ashore, the bewildered Hawaiians trying to understand what was happening. Within just 40 years of Cook's arrival, Hawaii began to feel the forces that would change it drastically.

"*T*he year 1819 was a pivotal one for Hawaii," said James Luckey, general manager of the Lahaina Restoration Foundation. "That year King Kamehameha died, the first whalers arrived in Hawaiian waters, and the first missionaries left Massachusetts for Hawaii. All those forces came together here." We were touring Lahaina, a little town on the west coast of Maui.

The main street was a congested mass of tourists, lured by a double row of shops and restaurants. Jim has been involved since 1972 in restoring and preserving Lahaina's historic structures. The entire town has been designated a National Historic Landmark.

"Many of the captains of the whaling vessels that called in Hawaii were stern Congregationalists," said Jim. "So rather than use the harbor at Honolulu—a city they considered as wicked as Sodom—they began anchoring here at Lahaina. But at one time there were 28 grogshops here on Front Street, so Lahaina probably wasn't much better than Honolulu."

Jim's latest project, which he proudly showed me, is the restoration of the Wo Hing Temple, the meeting place of a Chinese fraternal society

Native daughter of the islands, Elizabeth Chandler threads plumeria blooms into a lei. Numbering perhaps 300,000 in the 1780s, pure-blooded Hawaiians have been reduced to fewer than 9,000 by disease and intermarriage.

dating from the early 20th century. Chinese gentlemen once came to the two-story wood-frame building to gossip and to smoke opium.

Down the street we stopped at an old stone structure, the U. S. Seamen's Hospital, built in 1833. "When Kamehameha died he was succeeded by one of his sons—Kamehameha II," said Jim. "He and his queen both contracted measles during a visit to London in 1824 and died there within a few days of each other. Another son, a youngster, became Kamehameha III. As a young man he liked to come to Lahaina, and he used the Seamen's Hospital as a sort of hideout to get away from his advisers and guardians. Evidently there were some terrific parties upstairs here."

The carefully restored stone Baldwin House, the home from the mid-1830s to 1870 of Dr. Dwight Baldwin, one of the early missionaries in Hawaii, has a lovely, shady porch overlooking the harbor at Lahaina. Inside, several original pieces of furniture and some period antiques give the home a lived-in feel. In faded photographs on the walls, the missionaries scowl as angrily as the fierce Hawaiian gods they had come to combat.

The missionaries are still a somewhat controversial subject in Hawaii. On the one hand, they certainly contributed to the destruction of the Hawaiian culture, with what one historian called their "uncompromisingly

Wet and dry on Kauai lie just ten miles apart. Moisture-laden clouds drop 460 inches of rainfall on Mount Waialeale (above) each year. Carved by runoff from the mountain, Waimea Canyon (left) receives 20 to 40 inches.

FOLLOWING PAGES: *Glittering Waikiki Beach curves toward Diamond Head, where 19th-century British sailors mistook volcanic crystals for diamonds.*

righteous" behavior. With perfect confidence in the rightness of what they were doing, they stamped out the native songs, the dancing, and the nudity that were such a part of the islanders' lives. Historian Edward Joesting has written: "The great damage the missionaries did was an unintentional one, a harm they would have been hard pressed to understand. Christianity was a Western religion, and to be a Christian one had to have the conscience of a Western man. The Hawaiians were Polynesians, and the concept of Christian sin missed the Polynesian mind." He called the Hawaiians "a maimed race destined to an unhappy fate."

On the other hand, the Hawaiian culture would have collapsed in the face of the Western onslaught in any case. One 20th-century native minister, the Reverend Abraham K. Akaka, wrote: "I am glad that these missionaries, so often ridiculed and maligned, came to our islands and to our people. Because of them, we native Hawaiians have fared much better over the past one hundred and fifty years than 'discovered' natives in Africa, India, the Americas, and other areas of the world. Rather than bringing extinction and extermination, the missionaries were a people who . . . brought joy of heart and gladness of soul."

The first white child born in the islands was a missionary's son, Levi Sartwell Loomis. The English doctor who delivered the baby on July 16, 1820, would not accept a fee, so the father gave him, in appreciation, an edition of Milton's *Paradise Lost*.

Fragrant and fragile leis hang in a Honolulu shop. Each may contain 450 individual blossoms. Leis date from ancient times when, Hawaiians say, gods strolled through island forests decked in garlands of flowers.

Perhaps paradise was not quite lost, but it was slipping away. In less than a century the number of native Hawaiians was reduced by 75 percent—from 300,000 in Cook's time to about 70,000 in 1850. Diseases and whiskey introduced by the Europeans made short work of entire villages.

Toward mid-century Dr. Baldwin treated a patient for what he thought might be the dread *ma'i-Pākē*—Chinese disease. We know it as Hansen's disease, or leprosy. It's uncertain where leprosy came from, but once in Hawaii it spread alarmingly. In 1865 the Hawaiian legislature authorized the segregation of the victims from the rest of the population, and Kalaupapa, a flat peninsula on the north coast of Molokai, was chosen as the site for a colony. A sheer cliff cut it off from the rest of the island, and rough seas made it difficult for ships to land. For nearly a hundred years the afflicted were sent there. Often, they were thrown overboard and forced to swim ashore. At first they were expected to look after themselves, and no provision was made for their care. Since there was no cure for leprosy, they had been sent to Molokai to die. A state of anarchy existed there, and drunkenness, rape, and robbery were not unknown. The misery and suffering of those at Kalaupapa must have been barely endurable. An early visitor called it "one of the most horrible spots on all the earth."

Things are much better now, of course. Modern drugs don't cure the disease, but they arrest it, and afflicted people can lead fairly normal lives.

Once, the only way to reach the settlement, other than by sea, was by a steep, narrow trail carved into the face of the cliff. Today there is a small airstrip at Kalaupapa, but many visitors still choose to ride mules down the cliffside trail. So that's how I came to find myself one hot summer day astride Pokane—Dark Night—a placid but shifty-eyed mule.

Along with 30 or so others, we descended the rocky, dusty trail through dense forest. Down and down we went, for an hour and a half, accompanied by the clatter of hooves, the laughter of inexperienced riders, the sound of the wind in the trees. A short ride along the beach brought us to a stand of trees where Henry, one of the patients still living at Kalaupapa, met us in a van. A boy of 15 when he was brought to Kalaupapa in 1941—three months before the attack on Pearl Harbor—Henry was a jovial and friendly guide, his disfigurement from leprosy scarcely noticeable. The day was warm and quiet, and so was the neat little town. Simple wood-frame houses, tidily kept, looked deserted, and many were.

"Patients can leave Kalaupapa now if they want to," Henry said, "but many have lived here for so long that this is their home. They're reluctant to leave. Most don't have anywhere else to go anyway. About a hundred remain." There is a small store—where we stopped for a soda—and the patients get monthly checks from the government for their support. "Kalaupapa has been designated a National Historic Monument," Henry told us, "and there are plans to make it a national park when all the current residents have passed on."

We visited a lovely little church—St. Philomena—that was one of several built by Father Damien, a saintly Belgian priest who came here in 1873 to work—and to die, 16 years later—among the outcasts of Molokai.

During that same century the foundations were being laid for Hawaii's economic future. Whaling was in decline by the 1860s, as petroleum began to replace whale oil, and sugar began to assume a new importance. Sugarcane had been brought to Hawaii by the *(Continued on page 174)*

Mule-borne trekkers descend the precipitous north coast of Molokai, where waterfalls thread steep pali—*cliffs (opposite). The rugged north is home to the sons of Joyce Kainoa (upper); she chose the area for its remoteness, hoping to re-create here the uncomplicated life-style of her ancestors.*

FOLLOWING PAGES: *Polynesian fantasy comes to life on Molokai, as tropical heavens blaze and slender coconut palms lean toward a setting sun.*

early Polynesians, and for years there had been efforts to farm it commercially. But it was the gold rush in California, which opened up a big new market, and the Civil War, which eliminated southern sugar from all markets, that made sugar a major industry here. At the same time, the continued drop in the number of native Hawaiians meant a shortage of cheap labor for the planters. In 1852 a shipload of Chinese workers arrived, the first of many; the labor supply had constantly to be replenished as workers, after a spell in the fields, moved to the cities in hope of bettering their lives. Chinese, Japanese, Portuguese, Puerto Rican, Korean, Filipino—these and others have taken their turn in the fields, and all have gradually been assimilated into the Hawaiian population.

That assimilation was not always easily accomplished, for, as historian Lawrence H. Fuchs pointed out, each group had different aspirations, and the white elite, the *haole,* wanted control. "The Portuguese longed to be haole; the Hawaiians dreamed of recapturing the past; the Chinese sought economic independence; but the Japanese wanted more than anything to be accepted for what they were—immigrants from Japan in Hawaii." Years later, after the attack on Pearl Harbor, the Japanese in Hawaii would suffer abuse and discrimination.

In the early 1900s James D. Dole successfully canned a pineapple in Hawaii, and another important industry was born. By mid-century, Hawaii was producing practically all of the world's pineapples. They have declined in importance recently as Brazil, the Philippines, and other countries have begun to compete, but there are still a lot of pineapples in Hawaii. About a sixth of little Lanai is devoted to their production.

When Lloyd Cockett showed me Kamehameha's fishing spot on Lanai, he also showed me pineapples, for there is no escaping them. There are rows and rows of pineapples, acres and acres, fields and fields, miles and miles of pineapples. Millions of pineapples. There are more pineapples on Lanai, it seems, than the planet can possibly use.

"Dole used to let all the islanders pick all the pineapples they wanted for themselves," said Lloyd. "But people abused that privilege, naturally, so now we're supposed to leave them alone. Maybe they won't mind if I harvest just one."

From a roadside clump, Lloyd selected a plump pineapple. He whittled away the hard skin and shaped a handle out of the stiff leaves and gave it to me—a sort of pineapple Popsicle. It was delicious, but impossible to eat neatly. In half a minute I had juice all over my face, all over my hands; I was up to my elbows in sweet, sticky pineapple juice.

James Dole's cousin, Sanford Dole, became the first president of the Hawaiian Republic when he and several other businessmen engineered the overthrow of the monarchy in 1893. Queen Liliuokalani, the last monarch, had reigned only two years. The 1893 revolution led to the annexation of Hawaii by the United States in 1898. It was a U. S. territory until it became our 50th state in August 1959.

Sugar and pineapples have about had their day in Hawaii. Since World War II the military has also been of vital importance to Hawaii's economy. In 1983 there were 26,000 service families stationed in the islands.

But the prime economic fact of life in Hawaii today is tourism. The history of just one government agency illustrates two things: the relentless growth of tourism over the years, and the increasing sensitivity of the

Life in a company town endures on Lanai, a Hawaiian island owned almost entirely by Castle & Cooke, Inc. Ernest Richardson (below) bids farewell to his wife, Rebecca, before a ride, and young Na Kala Kehaulani Mano grins shyly from her front steps. Virtually all of the island's 2,000 inhabitants live in Lanai City, and about 600 work on the Dole pineapple plantation, now run by Castle & Cooke.

Hawaiians to it. In 1903 a Joint Tourist Committee was formed. It soon changed its name to the Hawaii Promotion Committee, which became the Hawaii Tourist Bureau in 1919, which became the Hawaii Travel Bureau in 1944, which became the Hawaii Visitors Bureau in 1945.

The bureau's job is to keep the world's tourists interested in Hawaii, and judging from the results it's doing a fine job. In 1984 about 4.5 million people visited Hawaii, an area just twice the size of Yellowstone National Park. On any given day there are more than 100,000 tourists in the islands. The one million residents are nearly overwhelmed by this flood. There are now, in effect, two Hawaiis—one for the Hawaiians and one for the tourists—and they seldom meet. Visitors rarely see the "real" Hawaii, and Hawaiians do what they can to avoid being flattened by the tourist juggernaut.

It's a juggernaut that leaves behind a great deal of money in the islands—about four billion dollars in 1983. That same year, tourism generated 477 million dollars in state tax revenues and supported 164,500 jobs. Japanese tourists spend two and a half times more than U. S. mainlanders, so the visitors bureau now has a staffed office in Tokyo.

One of the first tourists to reach Hawaii was also, I think, one of the most interesting. Isabella Bird, a middle-aged Englishwoman with a bad back,

Protective gear shields pickers from the spiky leaves of pineapple plants on Lanai. Castle & Cooke devotes 16,000 acres here to the crop (above). For decades, immigrants recruited to labor in the fields have bettered their lot by moving to cities, there adding to the rich ethnic mix of our 50th state.

visited Hawaii in 1873 and wrote a series of letters home to her sister that were published as *Six Months in the Sandwich Islands,* as they were then known. Curious and fearless, but always a lady, she toured the islands pretty much on her own. Arriving on a new island, she would buy a horse and hire a guide—when necessary, one who spoke no English—and set off to see the sights. She thought palm trees looked "as if they had never been young," and found lava lying "in hummocks, in coils, in rippled waves, in rivers, in huge convolutions, in pools smooth and still, and in caverns which are really bubbles." The fresh-flowing lava at Kilauea was "fiery waves upon a fiery shore . . . and the colour! Molten metal has not that crimson gleam, nor blood that living light! Had I not seen this I should never have known that such a colour was possible." She marveled at surfers, sampled poi—"sour bookbinders' paste"—and urged her terrified horse across rain-swollen torrents. "Hawaii is all domes and humps," she wrote, "Kauai all peaks and sierras." She grew very fond of the Hawaiian people. "Used to the down-trodden look and harassed, care-worn faces of the over-worked women of the same class at home and in the colonies, the laughing, careless faces of the Hawaiian women have the effect upon me of a perpetual marvel." She wondered: "Is it always afternoon here?"

*I*n 1915 *The Aloha Guide,* which called itself "the first book of the kind" for the Hawaiian Islands, was published in Honolulu. Those were the days when first-class steamer fare from San Francisco was 65 dollars and rooms in Honolulu's dozen or so hotels cost two or three dollars a night; boardinghouse rooms were about ten dollars a week. The guide praised the Hawaiian people and the climate, and listed "sea-bathing" and "surf-riding" among the activities. "As we approach the pier," the author informed steamship passengers, "native boys swimming in the harbor and diving for coin will next attract attention." The Moana Hotel was located at Waikiki Beach, "about 31/2 miles from town." The guide noted the "calling days" for ladies, but warned, "The extensive use of automobiles has introduced harassing road construction problems." It listed the sight-seeing possibilities in Honolulu and called Pearl Harbor "a magnificent body of water of vast expanse." It touched only briefly on the other islands, for travel conditions on them were still primitive. But it did urge visitors to take day trips to the Big Island and to Maui, to see Kilauea and Haleakala craters. It called Lahaina "a sleepy village strung out along the shore."

Even in the 19th century, however, Honolulu was becoming a cosmopolitan city. "Honolulu in 1820," wrote a great-granddaughter of early missionaries, "had everything to sell that you could have found in the crossroad store at Brookfield or Cornwall or on the water front at Boston." Today it has everything to sell, period. A high-rise city of 780,000, it has many of the problems of other modern urban areas, but some amenities of its own, too. I happened to arrive during Aloha Week, a festival that grew out of an old-time autumn celebration following the harvest and the paying of taxes. Each island observes Aloha Week in its own way. In Honolulu, there's a lavish parade, an even more lavish Royal Ball, an outdoor crafts fair, concerts, talent shows, and magicians, clowns, and mimes. I sat one evening on the grassy lawn of the Iolani Palace for a band concert. Built in the late 1800s for a Hawaiian king, it is the only royal palace in the United

States; Queen Liliuokalani was imprisoned there briefly in 1895. The Royal Hawaiian Band, established in 1836, played in a gazebo-like bandstand beneath the trees. Their selections all had something to do with Hawaii, even the "Cosmopolitan March" by Victor Herbert, performed, according to the director, in honor "of the ethnic mix of Hawaii."

Later that night the city closed off Bishop Street, and a radio station played big band recordings from the '40s. People who would have been teenagers back then jitterbugged in the street. "Don't sit under the apple tree with anyone else but me," sang the Andrews Sisters, and Dick Haymes warbled "I'll get by."

The next day, jitterbugged out, I found my way to the renowned Bernice P. Bishop Museum. It is devoted to the culture and natural history of Hawaii and the Pacific. I strolled there in cool comfort among feathers and drums and whale-tooth bracelets.

The beach at Honolulu—Waikiki—is arguably the most famous in the world, its name a synonym for sun-drenched sand and surf since the days of Kamehameha, who enjoyed a day at the seashore as much as anyone. Today the beach itself is obscured by the towering hotels that line it. It's possible to stroll along Kalakaua Avenue, where the hotels are, and not suspect that you're anywhere near an ocean, so completely is it hidden. From poolside at the hotels, where white *(Continued on page 184)*

Garden of the Gods—an area of bizarre wind-sculptured formations—draws visitors to Lanai's interior. Each Hawaiian island typically has both rainy and dry regions, often separated by only a few miles, as trade winds out of the northeast deposit their moisture on windward coasts.

Haleakala—House of the Sun—rises 10,023 feet on Maui. Here silverswords thrive on sunbaked flanks (opposite), and clouds wash across lava boulders (upper). Cinder cones (above) pock the floor of the 20-square-mile crater.

FOLLOWING PAGES: *Sea and mist swirl through an ancient lava flow—a legacy of Haleakala on Maui's northeast coast. The volcano last erupted in 1790.*

pigeons loiter like the idle rich, you can look out at the sea. Surfers' dark heads bob in the blue distance, and kayak paddles flash in the sun. Snorkelers, spread-eagled and immobile, rock in the shallows.

On other islands, I sometimes surrendered to tour promoters and went where they wanted me to go, did what they wanted me to do. On the hot, dry western end of Molokai I rode in a van with some other tourists through the Molokai Ranch Wildlife Park. Giraffes rubbed their moist noses against the windows, and an ostrich paced angrily alongside. Barbary sheep, ibex, and axis deer watched from beneath scraggly trees and bushes.

Early one morning I went down to Hale o Lono Harbor, which each year is the starting point for an outrigger race from Molokai to Oahu, a distance of some 40 miles across open sea. Thirty-eight canoes were entered this year, and they were strung along the beach as their husky crewmen got themselves ready. At 7:00 a.m., someone blew a mournful note on a conch shell, and the crowd quieted. A minister prayed in Hawaiian, which made his prayer sound like a poem; in English, he told the participants, "You are at your best today," and thanked God for the Hawaiians' love of the sea. Then they were off, in a mad scramble of splashing and shouting and paddling. A team from Honolulu won, in 5 hours, 18 minutes, 19.62 seconds.

While visiting Hilo, on the island of Hawaii, I kept one eye on the crescent-shaped bay, for it was the site of at least two devastating tsunami. Because of its location and the configuration of the bay, the town seems especially vulnerable to these great sea waves. One, in 1946, killed 83 people when the water suddenly rose 30 feet. In response to that disaster, the county acquired the immediate waterfront area for a buffer zone. Demolished businesses reestablished themselves just back from it. Then, in 1960, the sea struck again.

A massive earthquake in Chile 7,000 miles away sent a surge of water racing across the Pacific toward Hawaii at more than 400 miles an hour. About 8:00 p.m. on May 22, sirens in and around Hilo went off, and people prepared for the worst.

James Hamasaki, then a county official, hitched a ride that night with a photographer for Hilo's *Tribune-Herald*. "We had been told to expect the tsunami about midnight," he said as we stood on a small highway bridge overlooking Hilo Bay. "But the first wave, which was noted about 12:15, was very small. A second, a half hour later, topped the seawall along Wailoa Estuary. I made every effort to escape the tidal action after taking some photos of the water gradually rising, raising the boats along with it. There were people everywhere. Many fled, and I was told that one person in the last photo I shot died. I was moved out of danger by a police officer."

Then, a little after 1:00 a.m., a 20-foot bore surged through the mile-wide opening in Hilo's breakwater. According to the report of the Army Corps of Engineers: "The massive wall flared out to strike the shores of the bay in different directions, rushed inland as far as 3,600 feet, and blanketed 550 acres of Hilo proper."

"I stood on a hill and watched the lights go out as Hilo filled up like a bathtub," said James Hamasaki.

In the morning, reported the Corps of Engineers, "Hilo was unrecognizable. A thick layer of mud covered the area, above which the air was impregnated with the stench of the city's disrupted sewer system. Many frame buildings had been reduced to splinters . . . 10- to 20-ton boulders had been lifted from the bayshore revetment and rolled hundreds of feet; asphaltic concrete pavements had been peeled from their subbases; hundreds of automobiles had been tossed around and crushed . . . heavy and light equipment, stock from commercial enterprises, residential furnishings, items of many descriptions and some beyond description were strewn about the devastated area. Where many concrete structures once stood, there remained only floor slabs . . . it took days to determine that 61 lives had been lost. . . . The total damages and losses conservatively estimated at $22 million."

Hilo learned its lesson. After cleaning up the rubble, the town turned the entire waterfront area into a park. In its center sits a somber memorial to all victims of tsunami, erected by a group of survivors. The park is a broad, green, peaceable place, the last vestiges of death and destruction long gone. There one Sunday afternoon I moseyed through a Filipino festival, balancing a paper plate of *adobo*—a sort of pork barbecue—and a soda. I made myself a little queasy eating too much macadamia nut brittle.

North of Hilo I strolled for an hour through the Hawaii Tropical Botanical Garden, a 17-acre nature preserve and sanctuary in a steep-walled valley. Its founder, Dan Lutkenhouse, retired from the trucking business in California and decided to devote the rest of his life and a good deal of money to preserving a place of rare natural beauty. He walked with me for a while, through the lush greenery of a primitive tropical rain forest within sound of the surf and downstream of a waterfall. "When I discovered this valley, it was densely overgrown but still spectacular. I fell in love with it," he told me. "In 1976 we started hand clearing to provide more than a mile of trails, built bridges, and created a large lily pond. Now we're planting different species of tropical vegetation from all over the world. We already have more than 680 species, including palms, bromeliads, gingers, heliconias, exotic ornamentals, medicinal plants, and even some endangered ones." It's Dan's goal someday to have specimens of as many kinds of tropical plants growing in the garden as he can find—and to preserve the valley for the enjoyment of future generations.

Some of the hotels in Hawaii are pleasure-domes as fantastic as Kubla Khan's. On the western coast of Maui, at Ka'anapali, I found one—the Hyatt Regency—that is a wonder. In its atrium, open to the sky, grows a 100-year-old, 70-foot-tall weeping banyan tree. Bougainvillea tumbles from the balconies toward the floor. On the grounds, nine artificial waterfalls pour 3,000 gallons of water a minute over a million dollars' worth of artificial rocks. There are 16,000 shrubs, 1,250 palms, and 1,300 other trees. But it is the wildlife that draws the crowds. There are, in the lobby and atrium, and on the grounds: African black-footed penguins, flamingos, Australian black swans, cockatoos, English mute swans, peacocks, Chilean black-necked swans, ducks, parrots, macaws, and 200 Japanese *koi* fish.

I looked up Kildee Jacobsen, an outdoorsy young woman in shorts and bush shirt, who is the Hyatt's full-time head of fish and game. She introduced me to some of her creatures.

In the atrium, a big blue macaw named Christopher sat on a perch. "A while back during a kona wind," said Kildee, "Christopher discovered that he could fly. He took off and spent a couple of days up the coast at the

Marriott." In one of the bars was Delilah, an African gray parrot of dubious talents. "Delilah can say 60 words, many of them not too nice, and can imitate the sound of a dog being hit by a car—barking, squealing tires, yelps." We approached a small yellow-and-orange parrot in a cage near the front desk. "This is Kuuipo," said Kildee. "She loves to be the center of attention and has found that if she lies on her back on the floor of her cage, the guests will think she's sick and make a big fuss. They go to the desk, and the desk calls me, and before you know it a crowd has gathered. That suits this silly bird just fine."

Later I helped Kildee put the birds away for the night. They "work" from eight to four every day and are glad when quitting time rolls around, according to Kildee. "Any overtime and they get stressed."

"The hotel spends about 700 dollars a month on food and vitamins for the animals," she said. "The nuts that Christopher eats cost four dollars a pound. I don't know of any other hotel in Hawaii that has a full-time fish and game department. And there's a vet on call who visits once a month."

Another day, still on Maui, I became the quintessential tourist and took a perfectly pointless but absolutely delightful trip down a volcano. It began early, when I was picked up by a van at my hotel along with half a dozen other tourists. We drove to a small beach park on the coast of Maui, where

Windsurfers take to the sea at Ho'okipa Beach and sunbathers to the pool at the Hyatt Regency, both on Maui. For many years, off-the-beaten-path Maui received few visitors. In 1959 the island could offer travelers just 750 hotel rooms; by the early '80s that number had exploded to 11,500.

we breakfasted on papayas and sweet rolls. Then back into the van for an hour-and-a-half drive to the top of Haleakala Crater, where the air, at 10,000 feet, was thin and cold. Clouds rolled in, dissolving as they entered the volcano's dry, dusty caldera. We got out of the van, put on helmets, gloves, and Windbreakers, and each of us picked out a bicycle. Yes, a bicycle, for it's possible to ride from the top of Haleakala to the little town of Paia on the coast, a distance of 38 miles, without pedaling once. It's all downhill.

Down and down we went, leaning into corners, our bells chorusing cheerily at oncoming traffic, down through a barren, rocky landscape, past the headquarters of Haleakala National Park, down into the warmer air and increasing vegetation, down past broad cattle pastures and through stands of trees, down and down, in and out of towns and across farms. Then we were at the beach, and it was over all too quickly.

Some days I rented a car and went off on my own, seeking out the more remote and isolated parts of the islands. Good highways lead nearly everywhere, though some, as they wind along seaside cliffs, require that you pay extra attention to what you're doing.

*T*he Hanalei Valley on the north shore of Kauai is still relatively undeveloped. Isabella Bird went for one of her rides here and wrote: "Indeed, for mere loveliness, I think that part of Kauai exceeds anything that I have seen." A quiet river threads a broad valley patterned with taro plots in every shade of green. From high on the valley's rim I watched cloud shadows drift across the valley floor, and the sun glint and sparkle on the water in the flooded taro fields.

Another day I drove along the south coast of Molokai to the island's lonely and rugged east end. A winding two-lane highway hugs the coast for about 25 miles, from Kaunakakai, the island's main settlement, to Halawa Bay. I drove and drove, creeping around hairpin turns, edging along sheer drop-offs, often moving at barely five miles an hour. As I rounded the end of Molokai, the land and vegetation began to change—I had moved into the rainy, windward part of the island. I turned on the windshield wipers to deal with sprinkles. Little streams tumbled down valleys around practically every bend. At Halawa Bay, the end of the road, a broad river crept down a lush valley, and rain forest climbed steep mountain slopes. At the head of the valley, far in the distance, two waterfalls—Hīpuapua and Moa'ula—scribed white gashes in the greenery.

A similar drive along the north coast of Maui led me to Hana on the island's eastern tip. Again, a narrow road followed the shoreline, slowing traffic to a crawl. A number of state parks and beaches offered stopping places along the way. At Hana, a quiet village still off the beaten path, I joined townspeople at their community center down by the harbor for a craft show, part of their Aloha Week celebrations. Hana had a population of about 3,000 in 1778; now there are around 1,500. A few miles beyond Hana are the Seven Pools of Ohe'o Gulch, in Haleakala National Park. The pools, where bathers splashed and laughed, are fed by a cold mountain

Kahua Ranch manager Monty Richards scales a high-tech windmill on the blustery Kohala peninsula of the Big Island—Hawaii. Three such towers produce two-thirds of the electricity used on the 20,000-acre spread.

Volcanoes on Hawaii yield fire and ice: Red-hot lava flows from Kilauea (left), and snow crowns 13,796-foot Mauna Kea (top). Several astronomical observatories on Mauna Kea scan the heavens. At Hawaii's latitude, the entire northern sky and 90 percent of the southern reveal themselves during the course of a year. Above, vegetation covers the collapsed roof of a lava tube—a conduit for molten rock from Kilauea 3,000 years ago .

stream and stairstep gradually down to the sea. Nearby is the grave of Charles Lindbergh, who loved Hana and chose it for his final years.

On the Big Island of Hawaii, the drive from the east coast to the west took me across the base of the thumb of land that juts from the island's north coast. This is the area of the Parker Ranch, at 225,000 acres one of the largest privately owned ranches in the world. Some of the countryside reminded me of parts of the continental Southwest: a sunburnt, rocky world of dry hills with scrubby grass and bushes. The ranch was established in the 1840s by a sailor, John Parker, who had left his ship some years before and gone to work for Kamehameha hunting wild cattle in the region. The king was born just north of here at Halawa on the windy Kohala peninsula. The road there climbs and climbs up to the crest of the Kohala Mountains, where, on the ridgeline, the wind always blows and the view, across the green hills and blue ocean, seems endless.

*H*awaii is indeed blessed with an exquisite natural setting—and the need to protect it increases as more and more people come to enjoy it. All of Polynesia will eventually face the same dilemma as tourists venture greater distances in greater numbers across blue horizons and into the far reaches of the Pacific. Let's hope the women of Fiji continue to hang garlands of sweetly perfumed frangipani around each tourist's neck. Let's hope the white flowers blooming atop Mount Temehani on Raiatea never become an endangered species. Let's hope Western Samoa remains an exotic and carefree realm. Let's hope the Tongan goddess Hikule'o can withstand the 20th century better than her Hawaiian counterparts.

One night in Lihue, on Kauai, my first night away from the shrill canyons of Honolulu and the gaudy clutter of Waikiki, I strolled down to the hotel's patio, mellow and replete with too much food and too much sun. I pulled up a chair on the fringes of a crowd and sat. A guitarist in a nearby bar was singing "A Rainy Night in Georgia." A newly arrived tourist murmured to his wife: "Can that be thunder I hear?" It was the surf.

Out of the shrubbery strolled a skinny cat, a tortoiseshell. She sprawled under a chair, but seemed distracted and restless. Her tail thumped against the ground. After a while I walked down to the beach and sat facing the ocean. Soon the cat came, too. She played on the beach, leaping and whirling, kicking up sand. I thought of Mehitabel, Don Marquis's fictional cat: "There's a dance in the old dame yet." A beach-bum cat, I thought. When she tired of playing, she came and climbed into my lap. The trade winds were strong and warm, ruffling my hair, making the palm trees sway. The moon made a broad path of dancing diamonds on the water, and the surf hissed and foamed at my feet. The cat, facing into the wind, laid her ears back and sniffed. Maybe she smelled fish and distant atolls and the rich, heady brew of Polynesia. Then she leaned back against my chest and began to purr a raspy little song of praise, content.

Opposites attract at Black Sand Beach on the southeastern shore of the Big Island, where creamy surf laps obsidian remnants of ancient lava flows.

FOLLOWING PAGES: *Lushness runs riot in a rain forest on Mauna Kea's windward slopes. Here giant ferns tower overhead, and flowers brighten treetops.*

NOTES ON CONTRIBUTORS

Since 1978, free-lance photographer PAUL CHESLEY has covered Death Valley, the Sawtooth Range, the Continental Divide, the Southwest, the West Coast forests, and natural wonders of Europe for Special Publications. His photographs have also been featured in NATIONAL GEOGRAPHIC and other magazines, and in the "Day in the Life of" series of books, including *A Day in the Life of Hawaii.* Paul comes from Red Wing, Minnesota, and has lived in Aspen, Colorado, for 16 years. Along with Nicholas DeVore and David Hiser, he is a founding member of Photographers/Aspen.

Born in Paris and raised in Aspen, NICHOLAS DEVORE III has done free-lance photography for National Geographic since 1972, and has contributed to the Special Publications *Life in Rural America* and *America's Magnificent Mountains.* His assignments have ranged from voyaging in a Micronesian breadfruit-tree canoe to shooting designer fashions, and his photographs have appeared in many U. S., European, and South American publications. Says Nicholas, "The trio from the Rocky Mountains regard *Blue Horizons* as their dream collaboration."

RON FISHER, born and educated in Iowa and now a resident of Virginia, has been writing and editing for National Geographic since 1970. He is the author of *The Appalachian Trail* and *Still Waters, White Waters,* as well as several children's books on natural history subjects and chapters in many other Special Publications. Ron's most recent book, the award-winning *Our Threatened Inheritance: Natural Treasures of the United States,* addresses issues surrounding national parks, forests, wildlife refuges, and other federal holdings from Maine to the Hawaiian Islands.

An Ohio native and a graduate of the University of Washington, DAVID HISER has called Aspen home since 1964; but he says "one of the nicest things about my profession is that I can live anywhere there is a telephone and an airport." Over the past 15 years he has taken photographs for more than 20 NATIONAL GEOGRAPHIC articles on subjects as varied as the Aztecs and Tasmania, the Pacific Crest Trail and Pitcairn Island. His work has also been published in numerous Geographic books, including *Splendors of the Past, Trails West,* and *Exploring America's Valleys.*

A connoisseur of islands, CHRISTINE ECKSTROM LEE contributed the chapter on the Virgin Islands in *Isles of the Caribbean* and was coauthor of *America's Atlantic Isles.* Since joining the National Geographic staff in 1974, she has also written about the Minoan civilization, the Adirondacks, the Great Basin, valleys of eastern North America, and the Natchez Trace for Special Publications; Judaism, Christianity, and Islam for *Peoples and Places of the Past;* and San Antonio for TRAVELER. A graduate of Mount Holyoke College, Chris lives in Alexandria, Virginia.

GENE S. STUART, a member of the National Geographic staff since 1978, has often written about anthropology and archaeology for young people as well as adults. She is the author of *The Mighty Aztecs* and several children's books, and coauthor with her husband, George, of *Discovering Man's Past in the Americas* and *The Mysterious Maya.* Chapters by Gene have appeared regularly in other Special Publications, most recently in *Exploring America's Scenic Highways.* A South Carolinian now living in Maryland, Gene is the Geographic's only honorary Samoan chief.

DAVID HISER

Craggy finger of Mount Otemanu rises above Bora Bora's crystalline lagoon, where fishermen ply the waters in an outrigger canoe. Centuries ago, canoes holding dozens of people and their provisions carried Polynesians on voyages of discovery across the Pacific.

ACKNOWLEDGMENTS

The Special Publications Division is particularly grateful to Dr. Yosihiko H. Sinoto of the Bernice P. Bishop Museum, Honolulu, and Professor Albert Wendt of the University of the South Pacific, Suva, for reviewing all the chapters in this book and offering many helpful suggestions during its preparation. We would also like to thank the individuals, groups, and organizations named or quoted in the text and those cited here for their generous assistance: Allen Allison, Isimeli Bainimara, Madeleine and Jean-Pierre Blavette, Moetau Boaza, Bob Boyd, Johnny Brotherson, Fergus Clunie, Robyn Coleman, Bengt and Marie-Thérèse Danielsson, Jan Eastgate, Jon W. Erickson, Tupou Posesi Fanua, Francis R. Fosberg, Malakai B. Gucake, Elizabeth Hahn, Ronald Hedani, Nane Herman, Hugo Huntzinger, Aaron David Mahi, Kura and Roger Malcolm, Sione Manu, Karen Murphy, James Parker, Patrick Picard-Robson, Tepoavae Raitia, Manoa Rasigitale, Van Richards, Deacon Ritterbush, Marie-Hélène Sachet, Francis Sanford, Maile Semitekol, Ewan Smith, Pomani Tangata, Bruno Ugolini, Takapuna Vaikai, Cordell and Juliette Varney, M. Christian Vernaudon, Jack H. Ward, and Paeru and John Whitta.

Library of Congress CIP Data
Main entry under title:
Blue horizons.
    Bibliography: p.
    Includes index.
    1. Oceania—Description and travel.   I. National Geographic
Society (U. S.).   Special Publications Division.
DU23.B56   1985   919.6'04   85-15507
ISBN 0-87044-544-8 (regular edition)
ISBN 0-87044-549-9 (library edition)

Index

Boldface indicates illustrations;
italic refers to picture captions.

ADDITIONAL READING

The reader may wish to consult the *National Geographic Index* for pertinent articles, and to refer to the following: Antony Alpers, *Legends of the South Seas;* R. Warwick Armstrong, editor, *Atlas of Hawaii;* J. C. Beaglehole, editor, *The Journals of Captain James Cook;* William Bligh, *A Narrative of the Mutiny on Board His Majesty's Ship Bounty;* Elizabeth Bott, *Tongan Society at the Time of Captain Cook;* John Carter, *Fiji Handbook and Travel Guide* and *Pacific Islands Yearbook,* 15th edition; Erwin Christian and Raymond Bagnis, *Les Îles de Tahiti;* Sidney Colvin, editor, *The Letters of Robert Louis Stevenson;* Ron Crocombe, *The South Pacific: An Introduction;* Bengt Danielsson, *Tahiti: Circle Island Tour Guide;* Gavan Daws, *A Dream of Islands;* A. Grove Day and Carl Stroven, editors, *A Hawaiian Reader;* Edward Dodd, *Polynesia's Sacred Isle,* vol. 3; Michael Drollet, *Cook Islands Directory & Guide Book;* William Ellis, *Polynesian Researches;* Abraham Fornander, *An Account of the Polynesian Race, Its Origin and Migrations;* Derek Freeman, *Margaret Mead and Samoa: The Making and Unmaking of an Anthropological Myth;* Kim Gravelle, *Fiji's Times: A History of Fiji;* William R. Gray, *Voyages to Paradise: Exploring in the Wake of Captain Cook;* Teuira Henry, *Ancient Tahiti,* vols. 1 and 2; Jesse D. Jennings, *The Prehistory of Polynesia;* Edward Joesting, *Hawaii: An Uncommon History;* Patricia Ledyard, *The Tongan Past;* David Lewis, *We, the Navigators;* John Martin, *Tonga Islands—William Mariner's Account;* John W. McDermott, *How to Get Lost & Found in the Cook Islands;* Ray Riegert, *Hidden Hawaii: The Adventurer's Guide;* Noel Rutherford, editor, *A History of Tonga;* David Stanley, *South Pacific Handbook;* Ian Todd, *Island Realm.*

Composition for *Blue Horizons: Paradise Isles of the Pacific* by National Geographic's Photographic Services, Carl M. Shrader, Director, Lawrence F. Ludwig, Assistant Director. Printed and bound by Holladay-Tyler Printing Corp., Rockville, Md. Film preparation by Catherine Cooke Studio, Inc., New York, N.Y. Color separations by the Lanman Progressive Company, Washington, D. C.; Lincoln Graphics, Inc., Cherry Hill, N.J.; and NEC, Inc., Nashville, Tenn.